WHEN THE F

WILL HE TEXT?

And How to Know if He's Worth the Wait

JACQUELINE KRAVETTE
SARA ONEIL

FINN-PHYLLIS
PRESS

Copyright © 2021 by Jacqueline Kravette and Sara ONeil

Published by Finn-Phyllis Press, Inc.

All rights reserved. No part of this publication may be repro-
duced, in whole or in part, in any form or by any means,
electronic or mechanical, including photocopying, recording, or
by any information gathering storage and retrieval system now
known or hereafter invented, without written permission from the
publisher.

Cover design by JetLaunch.net

When the F Will He Text / Jacqueline Kravette & Sara ONeil
-- 1st ed.

ISBN 978-1-7359743-8-5 (paperback)

ISBN 978-1-7359743-9-2 (eBook)

DEDICATION

This book is dedicated to every woman who has felt slighted, ditched, ghosted, abandoned, gaslit, shamed, used, abused, or cast aside.

It's for every woman who has been dumped, cheated on, or replaced.

It's for those in pain and who may be heartbroken or confused.

It's for those left wondering or waiting.

This book is for you.

From our hearts to yours. We get it.

It's our wish that you will soon see what we do.

xo

We are writing this book from our experience. As women, we have obsessed over men: the men who weren't texting, calling, or DMing us on Instagram. The men who left us in a perpetual state of self-induced limbo. We've spoken with innumerable females who've also experienced this curious predicament. We have also talked to straight men and the LGBTQ+ community about their dating experiences. This book intends to leave no one out, and we hope everyone will read these pages and glean the message of energy and freedom offered. Energy is energy, and love is love. But we must write from the place we know best, which is that of women who date men, so that is what we have done.

May you find both yourself and a renewed sense of hope in these pages.

All names have been changed so as not to mess with the law of karma.

Love,
Sara and Jacqueline

CONTENTS

INTRODUCTION

L ove. It's the most heart-pounding, thrilling emotion on earth and better than any drug imaginable (not that we've tried them all). When it's reciprocated, it's the closest thing to unadulterated heaven on earth. Or it can be one of those upside down, inside out, backward, and sideways rollercoasters that makes you bargain with God about being willing to do a lifetime of charity work if you can just get out alive. Perhaps even worse, when love is taken away, the resulting pain can make the toughest mofo on the planet fold like a house of cards.

There are a lot of books out there about love—how to get it; how to keep it; how to recover it if it's lost. Most of us have read *The Rules, Why Men Love Bitches*, or *Men are from Mars, Women are from Venus* as if it were holy scripture, praying that allegiance to the newest time-tested methodology would prove useful. You can walk into any bookstore (okay, there are fewer and fewer bookstores these days, but the visual is better than one of mindlessly scrolling through Amazon) and find entire sections on the topic.

Our own secret book stashes, which were of course hidden behind our nightstands from any future potential suitors, provided us with some of our favorite one-liners:

"He's in his cave. Let him do his thing…he'll be back."

"Men are hunters. Never chase a man."

And of course, the standard best advice: "Ignore him; he'll come chasing."

They all offer perspectives and facts to women frantically trying to figure out if their guys love them as if they were doling out snacks at recess. But truth is truth, and it will continue through the ages.

A popular book in the early 2000s slammed that truth right in our faces: *He's Just Not That into You*. There was nowhere to turn or hide from that message, and we loved and hated that book. Its pages handed reality to generations of love-stricken females as they roamed the earth looking for signs that "he likes me back." There is something freeing, albeit devastating, about knowing that if he isn't calling, he just isn't into you. It's simple, clear, direct. Here is the problem: Women are sensitive. We feel. We love to talk. And most of all, we need some damn hope.

Sometimes, getting knee-capped with a baseball bat (metaphorically speaking, of course) is too harsh. We need a hot minute to wrap our heads around a situation. We want to hash it out and talk for hours about every comma used in each of his last forty-eight texts. We need this time to precisely comb through each possible scenario and reiterate plausible options over and over (and over) again to even begin coming to terms with the reality that he might, perhaps, not be that into us. While being punched in the face with an unforgiving truth may work for men (and some women), most of us need to slog through all the details. We must do this to ease into the idea that Mr. Fucking Perfect is perhaps…not.

Some books will rip off that hot, dirty, 6'2, fully sleeved Band-Aid with a yank that would rattle the stoicism of Queen Elizabeth, but we've found that women prefer the Band-Aid be removed via more of a gentle tug. We may have been dating a womanizing man-child who lives in his grandparents' basement. However, we still need to know that he MIGHT come back and COULD confess his undying love at some point (even though every single person in our life may be clutching prayer beads, chanting for him never to return). Perhaps you indeed know deep down inside that he isn't coming back, but this small window of hope is required. It allows you time to adjust, handle, and cherish the treasure trove of gifts that this heartbreak—yes, we said heartbreak—will bring you.

We don't know why any man has or will come into your life. Is he your future groom who will espouse his love for you on a beach in Maui? Or is he your catalyst for change, a change that will ultimately bring about your long-term "plus one?" Only time can paint the final picture we all desperately want to hang on our dining room walls right now.

The structure of this book is simple. We'll delve into the how-tos, the what not to-dos, and a few other tidbits you've maybe already heard. The key is that every concept mentioned in the following chapters has been tried, tried, and tried again. We have, even against our own wishes and desires at times, attempted all approaches repeatedly. The result was lessons that have been handpicked to be plunked down on the roadmap to true and lasting love.

Not much *hasn't* been written, sung, painted, or said on this subject. Everyone from Shakespeare to Patty Stanger has offered their take. This is ours. And if we may say so ourselves, it's pretty good. We have both tirelessly struggled to smash these theories into pieces and prove that they are wrong, but dammit, we can't.

We all fumble through life and relationship challenges. However, we firmly believe in "paying it forward," and the lessons learned during the dating process need to be passed along from one woman to another. Our experiences became these principles. And although we believe there is no right or wrong in this area (or any area of life, for that matter), there is such a thing as squandered time. That is what we hope to help you avoid by slicing off some of the learning curve.

Sara's initial writing of this book in 2007 had more fluffy, flowery words and horrible grammar. Sara and Jacqueline wrote a second version of it in 2013, which was too perky and optimistic—but slightly better grammar. But the quintessential "strong guidelines" were exactly the same! So, we are either greedy for taking so long to get this out into the world or slow AF. Perhaps both?! But here it is—same message, different decade.

Sara stumbled upon these principles through trial and error after a brutal breakup as the world nervously tipped into the year 2000. She applied them enough times to determine that they were accurate and then followed them almost perfectly from that point forward (littered by multiple lapses, as well as more than a few attempts to prove them wrong). Despite desperately not wanting them to work, she intuitively knew they were infallible.

Jacqueline, however, had a different journey—a long one. When she and Sara met in 2002, Jacqueline was in a full-blown love-addicted downward spiral. She was fighting with another woman (with whom she remains friends to this day) to win over a man who was basically living in a homeless shelter in downtown Los Angeles. *He* couldn't decide between the two women. Jacqueline, stubborn and committed to a fault, hung in there to win her supposed Prince Charming. Not unlike a drug addict, her need for him to be her guy was so intense, so profound, that she was willing to lose everything to win him.

After twenty years of failed attempts at proving that there was a different way to reach success in love than adhering to these principles, she acquiesced. And believe us, she tried every which way to find the loophole that would allow her to do it her way.

Nope. No dice.

We encourage you to have hope that your story can be the exception to the rule. We do not want or need to be "right." We are not here to shove any philosophy down your throat. You might hate what we say and set out to prove us wrong. We encourage you to do that! But please note in advance: We've found that women often put forth great effort in retaliation against these ideas, only to later admit to having that screechy voice within all along whispering, "Bitch, you know it's true."

If a point we make resonates with you, great! If it feels unquestionably wrong, pay attention to that feeling. If you do find that you want to punch one or both of us square in the face, we invite you to dig a little deeper before throwing out the book (in the proper recycling bin, of course). Each time we have desperately committed to justifying why an approach or an explanation was not for us, it was generally because we didn't want to admit that it was, in fact, very much for us.

Your desire to have him, her, or whomever may presently be stronger than the effort it takes to try these approaches. We get it. Do your thing. We will happily wait. And we will still be here, if and when you decide that you need a new tactic.

CHAPTER ONE

WELCOME BACK!

Is there really anything new to say about love? Perhaps not. But maybe.

In general, life is like the early bird buffet special at Ponderosa—there are endless choices. Is love any different?

The ideas, pontifications, and examples throughout this book come from our combined fifty years of real-life experiences. This is not an amalgamation of the best dating self-help books we filed away over the years and then regurgitated ten years later. Each lesson and moment arose from countless attempts, tears, successes, failures, and laughs. We have employed every word you will read in the following hundred plus pages. Some approaches were easy to try, almost effortless, in fact. Mostly when we thought we were exhibiting said approaches to get what we wanted, AKA HIM. Others took decades to successfully implement following train wreck after train wreck.

We want to inspire you to truly know how fantastic you are—which can be easily forgotten while waiting for XYZ to call. We want you to choose YOU. It is our opinion that when we humbly (and embarrassingly) show you our flaws and missteps (okay, complete screw-ups), you will realize that you aren't alone and more easily let go of any erroneous feelings of failure or imperfection.

Developing as women is a process, and we don't always "get it" entirely or all at once (spoiler alert: there is no such thing as perfect). What one might see as a success, another might not consider successful at all. As long as we measure our journey by our personal barometers, we are on the right track. If, on the other hand, we compare ourselves to the Angelina Jolies of the world, we begin to believe that we, too, should have Brad Pitt and a soccer team of kids to be happy. But in case you missed it, even Angie has love challenges and Brad is no longer in the picture.

This book will sometimes divert to Sara's or Jacqueline's experience specifically because, as you will see, our experiences have been entirely opposite one another's. Together, we can cover almost every scenario imaginable. Both of our journeys and encounters were perfect for our unique lessons and growth, and we believe you will most likely find a part or all of your story in one of ours.

Let's choose our own damn happy ending, shall we?

The approaches in this book unquestionably work if you listen to and apply them. We'll show you our battle scars and the crazy places we have gone while chasing love for a particular reason. You might wonder, *What reason ever could have compelled you to put up with THAT?* We promise to get to it. Just stay with us.

We're not proposing that this book will eliminate your $250 an hour therapist bill, but it will help. Who knows, you may even be able to offer your therapist some tips. Crazier things have happened, and we know many therapists asking the same questions as you: "Does he love me" and "Will he call?"

We know the pain you are in. You don't pick up one of "these" books if that isn't the case. We, too, have felt our hearts break as our tears fell into our kale salads, so we know how much it sucks. There is nothing more frustrating than wondering if our feelings are reciprocated. It creates feelings that range from awkward and annoying to enraging and downright excruciating.

Life is short, and the years seem to fly by faster and faster the older we get. We hope to save you a little time and impart some of the hard-earned wisdom we've gleaned when it comes to dating, love, and finding The One.

Dive in and feel it out. Let's pretend we're having a cup of tea while dishing on our favorite subject...LOVE! (And questions such as "Is he the one?" "Does he like me?" and "How does he really feel about me?") Sound familiar? Thought so. We've got you.

So put down those tarot cards (we know you have them), cancel that psychic appointment, and let's go on a journey together.

CHAPTER TWO

SHIFT YOUR FOCUS

R epeat after us: I am awesome. I am confident. I am fearless. I am sexy. I am hot, and men fall at my feet.

Don't worry, this book is NOT that!

We are definitely *not* going to recommend that you spend hours staring at your Post-It-Note-affirmations-covered mirror trying to hypnotize yourself into some bullshit state of mind that leaves you the moment you step into your kitchen. In fact, we're the girls who do our best to avoid the "how-tos" and the "must-dos" typically included at the end of relationship book chapters. We rarely do the recommended exercises (though we'll admit to having completed a few). And again, we most certainly didn't write this book because either of us has "Ph.D." after our names. Many (not most—we don't like to generalize) relationship experts are as screwed up in the dating department as the next girl.

At some point on this mad journey, we decided to stop waiting for Cupid and snatch that damn arrow for ourselves. Love may be a mystery, but we are not its bitch. There are some aspects of love that we can't control, but we *do* have the power to control ourselves! What does that mean? In its most straightforward breakdown: We can't control who else loves us, but we *can* love ourselves regardless. Our goal is to help you shift things on the inside so that your outside will do a doubletake.

What is the bottom line? Freedom. Freedom from needing things to go down the way that you think they should. Why? Because once you have that freedom, you will know that what is meant for you is truly meant for you. Too much too soon? No problem. More on that as we go.

Women are amazing, complex enigmas. Yet, despite our beauty, wit, and brains, we can lose sight of our essence the minute a man enters the picture. We have witnessed the smartest and most talented women shriveling up and disappearing because a particular man didn't return her affection—or, let's be honest, her text.

Why? Who knows! Of course, there are psychological reasons, but since we are not therapists, we will not be jumping into that (very deep) rabbit hole. We will discuss how not to lose who you are and what you want because some sexy dude in yoga class admired your warrior pose (downward dog seems a bit too on-the-nose). That naughty and out-of-reach bad boy or high-powered attorney with the summer house in the Hamptons is undoubtedly not having coffee at Mel's Diner, obsessing with his three closest guy friends about why you didn't snuggle for more than three minutes in bed the night before.

We consider ourselves to be reasonably spiritual, kind, smart, well-rounded people. After nearly constant bouts trying to fill ourselves up with "outside stuff" to feel good on the inside, it became clear that life truly is an inside journey. No size-four jeans, hot guy on our arm, or penthouse on Central Park West was going to make us feel complete. Nor would the Jerry McGuire "You complete me" lie of the century.

We spent years fervently seeking the spiritual answer. From Scientology (only Jaqueline can take credit for this one), Kabbalah and Shamanism, to shrinks and life coaches to psychics and self-empowerment courses, we have searched passionately for answers. In the end, it became clear that the fundamental nature of each of them was the same:

Along with the money and time spent seeking knowledge and blueprints on how to shift our lives into what we thought we wanted, we still did exactly what WE wanted to do.

We continued to apply what we wanted when we wanted. Period. We all do what we are going to do anyway. Even if the best therapist in Beverly Hills instructed you on exactly how to change your life or told you to immediately leave your current man, would you?

There is only one prerequisite to making impactful changes. It doesn't involve finding the perfect holistic getaway retreat center in Arizona where you can experience the yoga-filled, green-drink recharge that allows you to come back renewed. Instead, you must do one simple thing: Be honest with yourself. Ask yourself the million-dollar question: *Do I want to change?*

Forget what you know.

Forget what you think you *should* do.

DO YOU WANT TO CHANGE? Or, more accurately, do you want your experience when it comes to dating and relationships to change?

This is not a trick question. We know you're here because, more than anything else at this current moment, you desperately want to know if *he* likes *you*. But what if you had to shift some of your ideas/thoughts/beliefs around to get what you want. Not what you *think* you want, but what your soul *really* wants.

Would you do it?

Let us be clear. We are each the first to know what is right and wrong for ourselves and what we, therefore, "should" be doing. In fact, we are the *only* ones who know what is truly right or wrong for ourselves. Telling others what kind of monster they are if they do this or that is pointless because people do what they want to do. Therefore, if someone is worried about being judged, she will most likely conceal her choices from you. No one wants to be dishonest, but we hide because many of us don't want to be judged, disliked, or discarded.

We would love to tell you to run from everything not worthy of your precious time. But we are humble enough to acknowledge that we don't know what choices you should or should not make, so we won't tell you how to conduct your life. We would love to say, "He is a no...move on!" and save you that time. But we can only lead you to your own intuition and present you with the truth bombs that worked for us and others. From there, it is up to you. Upon hearing them, here are your three options:

1. Apply them (STAT) because life is too short, and you don't need to look any further to know the truth.

2. Acknowledge the truth but that it isn't quite time to act on it. This kind of investigation is good because you need to know your answers—for you and only you.

3. Decide, "Screw it. I know he's wrong for me, but I'm going to overlook it for now, and I don't care."

There are no right or wrong decisions, only consequences to those choices.

Jacqueline's Story

Steven, my most significant relationship teacher,
was why I sought out therapy twenty years ago. However, even with a Ph.D., it wasn't long before a
renowned counselor to the stars (someone who could
"help anyone" and had "seen it all") could not stand
me anymore.

He offered suggestions, hobbies, anything that
would distract my attention from Steven, who was
awful. Like, genuinely terrible. But to me, he was
JFK, Jr., risen from the dead. I said no to every amazing man who crossed my path and wanted to take me
out, and these were smart, handsome, sane, non-
sociopathic men. A couple of them were even famous.
It didn't matter. I was obsessed with obtaining the
love of the on-and-off drug-addicted, cheating, lying
con-artist I thought was my soulmate. After nine
months of attempts by my overpriced therapist (which
included him falling asleep not once, not twice, but
three times while I prattled on about this love of my
life), he found the phrase he'd continue to repeat for
the *next* six months:

Why do you care about YOUR life so little?

I dismissed him, as I did everyone who tried to steer me away from Steven. Two decades later, I finally understand what he meant. So, when it comes to relationship woes, and I say, "I get it," I don't mean that lightly.

CHAPTER THREE

WHILE YOU'RE WAITING… (TICK TOCK)

Janine spent three years thinking about Peter. She could have gotten her master's degree or graduated from law school in that amount of time. Natalie spent an entire year thinking about Chad's return. She could have written a book instead. Rene spent six months worrying about where Jonathan was throughout the day and whether or not he would call. During that time, she could have trained for and run a marathon. Kim spent an entire month wondering if Rick would call for a third date. She could have volunteered for the Boys and Girls Club and made a real difference in someone else's life.

Tick tock tick tock tick tock tick tock tick tock…

We can spend hours, weeks, even years obsessing

over a man. We wonder:

Will he call?

Does he like me?

Is he my future husband?

Where does he see this going?

When's the next date?

What did it mean when he said that he had a good time?

Simply put, if it's going to be, it *will* be, whether we obsess about it or not. If he is going to call, he will call. If he is going to be your future husband, he will (eventually) propose. We've all wasted quality moments that we could have spent being IN THE MOMENT. We've squandered time on men who were never worth a coffee date, let alone eighteen months of obsession. If someone is worth your time, he will be in your life without an avalanche of effort on your part. Claim your power. Be present. Do what will make *you* happy—whether he stays or goes.

Before we launch into a speech about the sacredness of life and how short it is, let us make one point very clear: Combined, we have wasted at least two and a half decades on does-he-love-me thoughts of flight and fancy. We have spent thousands of dollars on psychics and tarot card readers (no need to judge us, we judge ourselves), asking them over and over, "What's happening with so-and-so?" We have spent incalculable hours on the phone with girlfriends deciphering man codes. If all of this resonates, we are right there with you. We couldn't feel you more. We are also very aware that no amount of carpe diem talk we throw your way will stop you. It probably wouldn't have ever stopped us either, BUT…

It's like when you see an inspirational meme on Pinterest. The kind with a female warrior walking away from an explosion, above the caption: "Carpe Diem! Living for me." You get that surge of "Hell yes! If she can do it (on that meme anyway), so can I!"

That's what this is: a friendly reminder that life is short. Also, that if he wants to be with you, he will be (it bears repeating). And if possible, it's important to find a way to do something extraordinary while you wait for that damn phone to ding!

Of all the guys we obsessed over, none of them are with us now. Not that we haven't seen many cases where someone did come back. We have. The point is to try your best to warrior up and live your life in a badass way—*for you*. We want you to never look back and shame yourself for wasting years on that sexy comedian, the one who when you ran into him later, needed reminding of who *you* were.

On that note…tick tock.

CHAPTER FOUR

HOW DO I WAIT?
(THE MILLION-DOLLAR QUESTION)

This past week, we have had conversations around the same topic every single day. And not once every day but three times today alone. The particulars vary, but here are some one-liners from a few of them:

"He says he wants to move in together because school has been canceled (quarantine times) but wouldn't want to if he was going to school."

"He called at 4:30 yesterday, but that was the latest. Today he sent a few texts, but now I see him on Instagram, and he hasn't called to say goodnight."

One more we'll pull out of the hat:

"I met the hottest and most perfect guy in the universe, and we had sparks flying." (I'm paraphrasing this. It was initially said in a much cooler way.) "But I haven't talked to him in a couple of days. What does that mean?"

In each case (no different from the conversations we've had for the past twenty years), our replies gave the same suggestion, albeit in different ways:

"Sit back and watch so you can see *who* he is and if he is your guy. If he's yours, that realization will flow to you. If he isn't, it will be obvious. Go live your life and have a great day."

Sara's millennial friend surprised her with her rebuttal.

"Okay, great. *How* do I do that?"

Great fucking question.

The missing key to an already high-angst, anxiety-laden dating maze can be summarized by this exact question: How the hell do you resume life when you are in the throes of "Holy crap! I think I've met The One. Does he love me? Or like me? Is this my guy? Is it mutual? Why hasn't he called? Or texted? He's been on Facebook, and he liked one of my posts on Insta, but he hasn't texted one emoji today. I know I should be working, cleaning, studying, or otherwise getting my ass off the couch, but I can't. I can't stop thinking about him. What's going to happen with us?!

When other people are in this maze, it seems ridiculous, but (as you know) it's an entirely different ballgame when *you're* the one in it. You sit watching the seconds on the clock tick by as you mindlessly try to watch *Game of Thrones* for the third time, thinking Daenerys and her dragons can distract you. It's like getting a cold; you forget how much it sucks being sick when you're healthy.

Something as sweet as the potential for love can bring up all of your abandonment issues, fears, and even outright terrors. Conversely, it can kick the desire for one particular guy into overdrive, needing him to call, set a date, and get on it already! Why the wait? Why the hesitation? Especially when you can see that he is on Instagram! Is he talking to other girls? And if not, why is he doing something so trite and meaningless when he could be talking to you?

It's easy to address these questions when you are *not* in this awkward/frustrating/almost torturous place, the washing machine spin cycle of crazy. We easily toss out phrases to our friends such as "If he doesn't call, it's his loss," "Whatever, next," or even the nails-on-the-chalkboard line: "There are plenty of other fish in the sea."

You may even feel this spin cycle of emotions when reflecting, reminiscing, or comforting a friend. We forget when we're not in it—hey, sometimes we forget when we're in it. Love amnesia is an actual thing. Well…it might not have been an actual thing until this point, but we are deciding that it is from this moment forward.

We will delve more into the differences between men's and women's behavior in Chapter 13, Consider Cats and Dogs (and Dolphins), which is all about how to live in that in-between, what-the-hell-is-this-thing-if-it's-anything-at-all universe. How can we live in the space when we don't know what's happening or whether we will ever talk to a specific person again?

Sadly, there is no one right answer to this dilemma. Tricking the universe into thinking you have "surrendered" doesn't work either. We've tried. Saying, "Universe, I turn this over. I no longer care," and then quickly checking your texts to see if it worked does not qualify as a surrender. Sorry, not sorry. That's why a guy comes back months later when it's too late—you put all that energy into him and then faked letting go of the situation while crying into your pint of Ben and Jerry's. Then, when you finally didn't care anymore about him...*boom!*...there he was. Cue the universal law of cause and effect in its purest and most irritating form.

We believe that we are sad, distraught, or even mildly clinically depressed because he hasn't called, texted, or acted the way we wanted. But we're a bit mistaken. Men do the thing we "need," and we get an immediate hit, Band-Aid, pause, or thrill. A drug addict needs one more hit of crack, and he is a-okay for a minute. This is, at its core, no different. Maybe this will resonate more: you know when you stand over the sink shoving chocolate pretzels or carrot cake in your face moaning as it slides down your throat. Same, but different. But it's a temporary hit. It's not true satisfaction but merely filling a void of some kind. There are many serious addictions in the world from which people lose their homes, jobs, and families. However, there are also less-destructive addictions that are simply the result of not feeling like yourself (and, therefore, not feeling enough). When that happens, it isn't any one guy's issue—it's ours.

But back to the million-dollar question: How do you go on with your day without constantly thinking about him, asking every girlfriend again and again if she has a gut feeling, and checking your phone every five minutes? How do you spend your day without ceasing to exist while waiting for him?

First, you must acknowledge that most of the work to be done is yours. You may realize that you are so panic-stricken that you need to face some of your issues with the help of a licensed therapist. Maybe you're already in therapy but need to amp it up or try an approach that's more trauma-related, like EMDR or somatic healing. Or perhaps you will realize that this was guy number fourteen with the same temperament, and you finally see that it could be time to check out a co-dependency program. Whatever you come up with (or not), the work is yours to do, and acknowledging that is undeniably the first step.

Second, stop trying to pretend that you aren't completely, insanely mad over him, whoever he is. It's okay. We have no judgment of the fact that you are so giddy you can't chop your carrots finely enough. Acknowledge and accept that you are livid that he has not texted in three hours and twenty-eight minutes.

Stop trying to forget about it. It doesn't work. Remember, that's the "fake surrender" approach. The truth is, you're obsessed, and it's okay!

Now that you've admitted and (hopefully) accepted that you're obsessed, do anything and everything you can to LIVE YOUR LIFE ANYWAY! Go for a hike, paint something, have a friend over, or watch a movie. Do something, *anything*, that's in the opposite direction of what you were previously doing. A more significant and appropriate fear to have than not getting the "him" of the moment is reaching the end of your life and realizing that you wasted five years thinking about Joey with the big biceps and adorable Pomeranian. Trust us, a year from now, you won't even remember his last name.

You've already lost years obsessing over random dudes thus far (admit it; we have too). Moving forward, vow to *move* while you fret. After all, those five years spent dreaming about Joey will be much more satisfying if you also spend that time writing the novel you've been talking about for eight years. Let your angst move you into action! No, you probably won't completely override thoughts of him (though who knows, maybe you'll get lucky), but you will at least have something to show for it.

Are we annoying you yet? Are you shaking your head while mouthing, "Duh, this definitely does not work"? We hear you. We don't refer to the "how" of getting on with your life as "the million-dollar question" just for fun. But know that if you can't snap out of it, it's time to snap *in*to something else.

Remember, if he is your guy, he will call, show up, and show you that he's your guy. You want the guy who wants to be there, right? You should never have to remind someone of your existence. If you do, he's not your guy. It's important to remember that guys go about life much differently than girls do. They focus myopically on the task at hand, whereas women are much better at multi-tasking. If he is not calling when you think he should, that alone doesn't mean he's not your guy. He could be reorganizing his toolset, fixing a fence, watching the news, or spending an inordinate amount of time on the toilet. There is no need to text him or otherwise follow up to remind him of your existence.

For the rest of this chapter, let's pretend that there is no "him," and there's no call you are waiting for. We know it's impossible to eradicate it from your mind completely, but here are some new things to think about instead. As many nutritionists say, "There is no need to eliminate a food altogether; just add in some vegetables."

What do you want to do in your life?

Who do you want to be OUTSIDE of a relationship?

If you found out that you had one year to live— what would your legacy be?

Which friends and family have you overlooked who might need a visit from you? Can you toss your phone in a drawer for a day and go do something you've never done?

Where do you want to travel?

What do you want to do, be, and have?

What do you stand for?

What would you fight for?

Write out the answers. Start thinking of your life separately from how it would look with this specific "him" in it! Don't worry. You can still visualize a partner, put pictures of him on a dream board, and clear out half your closet to manifest the eventual sharing of space when he arrives. You can put a lamp on the other side of your bed and add some fun coasters for his morning coffee. But for now, where is your energy being spent? Where is your time going? Toward him, obviously, but think back to yesterday. Tally up your waking hours. How did you spend them? How many of them were spent trolling his IG or chatting about him? Perhaps you spent four and a half hours on Pinterest looking at this season's fashion tips. What did you spend your time doing? Be honest with yourself and get specific!

Now, what can you change? Can you make a declaration *not* to go on Facebook for a month? Or a week? Or a day? How can you reclaim your time?

This is a fight for *your* life, for what you *can* control. You may not be able to eliminate the fantasy of the two of you eating croissants together in Paris, but you can keep writing your novel and only think of him during coffee breaks.

What do you want to achieve for yourself over the next year or two? We know that you hate that question because we did too. But *why* do we so loathe thinking about our goals and where we want to be? Because when we do, we're told that we need to start acting toward those goals, which will divert us from our vocation of choice: HIM.

We know you don't want to look back in five years (when you'll believe that it's too late to open those yoga studios) and beat yourself up over the fact that "random sexy dude number four" took up all your mind space. The real question: Is he worth your time in the long run?

We promise you that he is not paying a fortune teller to predict your future together. If he wants to know something, he will ask/call/text you. Men are pretty straightforward like that. But until he does, focus on YOU!

CHAPTER FIVE

EVEN GISELLE WON'T CHANGE HIM

We all have repeatedly been told that beauty is in the eye of the beholder. Logically, the idea that what someone finds beautiful, sexy, or cute is subjective, but when most women go down the Instagram comparison hole of filtered, touched-up swimsuit selfies, that notion quickly flies out the window. For the sake of this lesson, think of the most beautiful woman in the world (in your eyes), and picture her now. If you scrolled through her feed, your thoughts would probably go in circles as follows:

Who is in your mind's eye right now? Is it Zoe Kravitz? Gigi or Bella Hadid? Kendall Jenner? Giselle Bundchen, Cindy Crawford, or perhaps her daughter Kaia (depending on your age)? Bring her to mind.

But we digress.

When Jacqueline was much younger, the concept of a perfect-looking woman who would never suffer through heartbreak played out all over her grade-school bedroom walls. From floor to ceiling were plastered magazine cut-outs of supermodels, only re-inforcing the fact that Cindy, Claudia, and Kate had it better. Hence, when Steven (her greatest relationship teacher) was in rehab for the fourth time, broke up with her while in his ninety-day lockdown, and start-ed dating a peer he met in said rehab, she decided that her huge (in her mind) hips were the issue. And if that were the issue (not his pathological incapability of being honest or sober), then she could fix it.

The cost of liposuction: $5,000. Six weeks of hip-to-foot Spanx and a ton of bruising later, he remained with that girl from rehab, never to return to Jacqueline. She now sees that as a gift, but back then, it took five girlfriends to try (unsuccessfully) to convince her that expensive and painful body recontouring was not the answer. From that point on, she acknowledged and accepted that going to significant lengths to reach supermodel status neither gets nor keeps a boyfriend.

Sara vividly remembers being devastated over a guy named Brian (although she had to wrack her brain to even picture his face today). He told her that he didn't want to be in a relationship. It absolutely crushed her, and she was desperate to figure out what she could do to get him to want her. She was especially upset about this guy because he just got his third DUI, was carless, and lived at home with his parents. She felt like the ultimate failure. A guy with no car and living at home as a grown man didn't want her?! She cried to a friend whom she often asked for relationship advice.

She didn't mince words in her response: "This isn't personal. It could be Giselle."

"What the fuck do you mean, 'It could be Giselle?'" Sara asked.

Surely, she isn't talking about supermodel Giselle Bundchen. If she were in his life, he would obviously swoop her up off her feet, bring her roses, and profess undying love. While courting her, he would get his life back together, move out of his parents' place into his new home in the Hills, live happily ever after, and it would be all thoroughly documented on TMZ.

Of course, Sara believed that her friend was wrong. She honestly thought that the problem was HER. She couldn't get him to fall in love with her; he was rejecting *her* specifically.

When thinking about that guy you lost, want, pine for, or however else you'd fill in the blank, the all too familiar "If I only…" stream of thoughts begins to circle in your brain. You may know them:

"If only I lost twenty pounds and had a bigger ass, he would never leave."

"If I were a little bit taller. If I were a baller…"

"If only I were hotter, thinner, hipper, more fun, or more sophisticated, he would forever be enamored with me."

"If only I had a million followers and men used my posts as their personal inspiration to do their business, he would do anything to get me."

These thoughts loop in our heads as frequently as Donald Trump appeared in the press circa 2019. Some of us become tormented by the false ideas of who we think we need to be, and sometimes we attempt to manipulate our physical bodies to feel more secure—or is it just Jacqueline? To be clear, we do not judge anyone who tweaks her body to feel more emboldened. We are speaking specifically about what we do hoping that it will save us from our shitty self-esteem: countless hours at the gym; a trainer; a new dietician; or participation in any new cleanse, fad diet, or surgical removal of cellulite. We pour our lives into the next hottest get-thin-quick scheme and invest our expendable income on the latest beauty crazes. Many do everything in their power to stave off the inevitable: aging. We believe that if we can transform our appearance into a "perfect" one (which doesn't exist), we will magically get what we want. As appealing as it might be to believe that you somehow have control over a man's choices, it doesn't work that way.

In the end, we only wonder what we did wrong, why he didn't treat us right, and whether it was our fault that he cheated with his co-worker—the one who has 250,000 Snapchat followers. We think there's no way he would *not* adorn Bella Hadid with head-to-toe Gucci and take her to Tahiti. We further believe that while courting her, he would get his life back together and move out of his aunt's guest house into his new, clean, beautifully designed home in the Hollywood hills, where they'd live happily ever after.

Our society is obsessed with youth and beauty. We imagine that another girl, a prettier girl, or a chick with blowjob lips would be treated differently. If he were with Giselle (or Cindy or Kendall or Kaia), there's no way he *wouldn't* settle down, buy her diamond earrings, prepare a picnic, or at least text more frequently! The reality is, sure, he might do those things for a minute, but he will then fall right back into who he actually is. Why? Because it's who he is.

"But when I press him and explain over and over how being home all the time and not going out for special date nights bothers me, he does become romantic and agree to travel." Yes, you can force a man into the six-foot padded box you've constructed for him. You can plot, maneuver, and manipulate all available elements to sway him into doing what you want. However, at some point, he will revert to his true nature (or secretly resent you).

And what we are yelling to you (hence the all-caps) is, HE WOULD DO THE SAME TO GISELLE OR GIGI OR CINDY OR KENDALL!

We hear you clamoring, desperately holding onto the belief that you can squeeze yourself to become as close to Scarlett Johansen as humanly possible if only you try hard enough. You're thinking, "The problem is ME. I can't get him to fall in love with ME. I'M the one who isn't quite good enough to get this guy" (this guy without a car, an apartment, or a job!).

You think that if you can figure out a way to make it about you, you can then have some sort of control over the issue. You'll be able to dictate the outcome and his love for you. Although this is impossible, we'll hear you out. Perhaps some guy *will* step up his game for Scarlett; let's say that's true. That A-game will exist for a hot minute, and then he will revert right back to himself! We are going to hammer this one home if it kills us: HE IS WHO HE IS.

The problem is neither you nor Giselle nor Kendall nor Gigi. The problem is him. It doesn't matter whom he's dating or what he is doing; he will do what he is going to do. No matter whom he's dating, he will ultimately still be himself.

Are you following? In case we need to be clearer, let us be a bit more direct:

- If he is a cheater, he will cheat on you.
- If he is indecisive about his future, he FEELS that way.
- If he doesn't like to plan too far in the future, he likes freedom.
- If he is stingy with you, he is stingy with everyone.
- If he criticizes your body, clothes, and hair, he will critique another woman's too.
- If he doesn't like romance, there are no cheese platter picnics for another woman either.

In other words,

- A non-romantic dude who wants to split the check…
- A non-committal, polyamorous hippy who avoids commitment…
- An angry guy who hates his parents and doesn't want kids…
- A sad complaining artist who has "Nietzsche" tattooed on his forearm…

Will not suddenly become:

- A super romantic guy who surprises you with Michelin star restaurant date.
- A monogamous, wedding-planning yogi.

It doesn't matter who he dates or falls madly in love with; he will continue to express himself in the exact same way because that is WHO HE IS, which is, ironically, exactly what you want him to show you. You cannot contort yourself to make him behave a certain way. As one of many wise therapists once said to one of us, "Make sure you are going to a well with water in it if you want to drink."

"But my friend's boyfriend *did* leave her for a model, and they are still together," you say with some sass. Sure, that happens. Maybe he was meant to be with that girl. However, he is still who he is while he's with her!

To sum it up:

1. Who he is isn't your fault.

2. Find men who are already available and healthy.

3. It is not your job to fix or to change someone.

4. He will be the exact same person for another woman too.

You may not see it now, but one day you will be grateful you let go of his scraps.

CHAPTER SIX

IF HE CAN BE LURED...RUN

The rule we've dubbed The Cindy Crawford Rule suggests that you should be able to leave your man alone with any beautiful woman, and he will remain faithful. This is the ultimate test. Would your man remain loyal if you left him alone with, say, Kaia Gerber or Hailey Bieber or Kendall Jenner? If your answer is not a resounding "Hell Yes," take note. We can carefully construct a world that shields our man from the mere possibility that there is a woman out there who is more beautiful than we are—and who may also want him. Worse, there may be another woman he wants. So, we do our best to consistently look sexy, in shape, and coiffed in an attempt to ensure his loyalty.

But...IF YOUR MAN CAN BE LURED AWAY BY ANOTHER WOMAN, YOU DO NOT WANT

THIS MAN.

Women are insecure for a myriad of reasons, most of which are intangible. Perhaps they had poor role models growing up. Maybe their father or some man close to the family was unfaithful. Simply not being heard or having one's feelings validated as a young girl can set the stage for a $15,000 therapist bill once she reaches her twenties. Regardless of how "put together" a woman appears, her insides may be screaming ferociously for validation. If that insecurity is then tested with another woman she deems more beautiful, sexy, or appealing, her competitive need to win will upstage all rational thought.

When you are out with your guy, does his glance seem to linger a little too long at your petite, blonde co-worker? If so, don't be afraid to bring your hot friend—the one who always wears a top that shows off her perfect DD cleavage—around him. It will be helpful and a time saver to weed out the jerks in the beginning. Usually, when you are freaking out that he might want some other girl, you are simply concealing the fact that you know he isn't your guy.

Sara's Story

Brian (the guy with the DUIs who was living with his parents) taught me a lot. I hung around for a bit (as one does) to make sure he didn't come to his senses and want to commit. Since I hadn't listened to signs one, two, three (and now four), I received yet another. I finally got my wake-up call when his "girlfriend" emailed me because she'd read his emails. Apparently, the reason (other than being an asshole) he was non-committal was to keep me at a distance because he already had a girlfriend. I was the other woman. Discovering this is always so much fun (that is sarcasm, FYI). His "real" girlfriend thought I was getting in the way of making him *her* perfect boyfriend (in other words, "I" was the problem).

We get it. It's one Jagged Little Pill (thanks, Alanis), and it is hard—very hard—to see the reality of it when it first hits you. Here's the other bad news: Our first reaction (usually) is to either blame the "real" girlfriend or figure out how we can get her out of the picture. We know this stabs deeper than a flippant "don't blame her." This "other girl" can represent childhood abandonment or bring flashbacks of not being picked for dodgeball as a child. It is painful, but it is not her fault. She is a *huge* gift. We *want* to see if he wants to be elsewhere.

When we are threatened by the beautiful younger woman who happens to be precisely his type or his friend (the one who seems a bit too happy to see him during your weekend grocery store run), we turn into women on the warpath. As a lioness protects her cubs, so shall a woman try to stave off any potential competition. Ultimately, you do not want a man who would even entertain the idea of hitting on your friends (or anyone else, for that matter). When we realize these "other women" are gifts and not threats, we can begin to welcome the Cindy Crawford Rule more readily, which states your man doesn't have to be blind to other women, but he shouldn't be lured or swayed by them. We aren't saying he shouldn't see another woman's beauty. Hell, we do too! It's normal to notice that someone is beautiful or sexy, but the real question is, does he have a spark for her?

You know that spark. It's that look that happens when a man sees "her." It is the look that you are trying not to notice. It is the look you hope isn't there, but instead of welcoming it as a gift, you try to become prettier or thinner or whatever else to keep her (and anyone like her) away from him. It's the look that he should have for you, and you know whether or not it's there.

Sidenote: You might be thinking, "I thought this wasn't a book of rules but more of teachings." And yes, we suggested that you use them if you want or toss them if not. However, if your man wants another girl, there is no debating the fact that you are not the center of his universe, and dammit, we want that for you!

This is not an easy realization, and even being open to this truth is brave AF. But there is a clear distinction between a man who is trustworthy and one who is not, as well as a man who knows how to be respectful and tone down his "flirtatious" nature by choosing to lower those pheromone flames and one who does not. Is there a bit too much eye contact with the cute twenty-year-old waitress who's explaining the pasta special of the day? Because you are gracious, you are not going to embarrass yourself or him by telling the bitch to back up because you know that it's okay if other women find your guy sexy. That's not the issue. The issue is whether he reciprocates the flattery. If you are trying to ward off women from entering his sphere because you are afraid to see the truth, you likely already know the truth.

Let your sexy friends back into your love bubble. Fear not! They are gifts disguised in hot shorts. If they can take your man from you, you don't want him! We know this is easier said than done because you really, really, really like him and don't want to open your eyes to see what he might do. We have most certainly been there, and it definitely sucks.

Which leads us to…

CHAPTER SEVEN

LET HIM BE FREE AS A BUTTERFLY

Free as a butterfly" was a concept given to Sara by that spiritual healer in 2000. Nothing like starting the century with a bang! She held her hand out flat to show the visual for a take-off and landing spot for said butterfly. The concept of "Free as a Butterfly" feels a little cheesy now that we are edgier, ballsier, and less people-pleasing, but to honor the origins of this life-changing concept, it shall remain titled as such. If it were to be renamed, we'd call it LOVE IS FUCKING FREE.

In other words, this means that you cannot maneuver, connive, manipulate, buy, or otherwise create the love of anyone. More specifically, you cannot—no matter how committed you are—force anyone into a relationship with you.

You know the prayer:

If you love something, set it free.
If it comes back, it was yours. If it doesn't, hunt it
down and kill it.

We know (intellectually) that we can't force someone to walk down the aisle. It's not like we're tyrants, constantly pushing people somewhere they don't want to go. We're kind, nice women. But sometimes, in the crevices and recesses of our crafty brains, we believe we can manufacture the exact circumstances that will make him want to do whatever it is that we want him to do.

Sometimes, a girl is blatant about her intentions to "catch" a guy. She hooks up with him and claims him immediately, perhaps by moving him in, befriending his family and friends, or helping him out with every nuance of his life (whether he wants her to or not). Once he's met her there she continues down the nice girl road. She cooks him dinner every night, reaches BFF status with his sister, and two years to the day from his capture, they say their *I Do's* in her dream wedding—the one she planned with his mother.

And then, one morning three years later, he cuts into the pancakes she cooked as she's making more coffee, looks up, and says, "I'm not happy." Or he doesn't even give a reason and runs off with some bitchy girl from the gym, as the scorned wife screams on TikTok about how she did everything for him—HOW DARE HE!

Let's list some of the circumstances we orchestrate for a guy to know that we are both outstanding *and* indispensable:

- We help him get a job, apartment, book deal, or new puppy.
- We move him to his new place.
- We support him so he can go to law school.
- We take care of him when he's sick.
- We make him breakfast, lunch, and dinner.
- We take him on vacation.
- We help him figure out his life issues.
- We do his taxes.
- We lure him with hot sex.
- We tell him who he can or can't hang out with.
- We tell him when he needs to be home to fit our requirements.
- We peruse his Instagram and Facebook for threats (and grill him on them).
- We threaten that we will leave if he does anything we don't like.
- We monitor his emails and texts like we're his boss.
- We drive him around because he doesn't have a car.

We know you are giving, kind, and sweet. Don't worry. We will cover that more in chapter 10. And remember, that is precisely why we're writing this book—to remind you how awesome you are so that you can begin to claim this truth for yourself and (hopefully) make different choices based on it.

The issue is not your kindness. The issue is your attempt to energetically and physically maneuver someone to be in your life. We do believe that "manipulate" is the word we are looking for. We are referring to how you might (perhaps unconsciously) be guilting, and if we may be so bold, hoodwinking him into staying. Maybe you're afraid of seeing that he isn't fully there in the first place?

And now you scream, "BUT I AM SO NICE/KIND/AWESOME/SUPPORTIVE! How could he do that!"

Again, we agree. YOU ARE!

There is usually a pendulum swing when it comes to this topic. For example, we—Sara and Jacqueline—swing in entirely opposite ways (okay, that sounded a bit not as we intended). Jacqueline is the helper (she single-handedly took care of her terminally ill boyfriend for three years), while Sara needs no one and has anxiety if there isn't complete freedom to go wherever she wants, whenever she wants.

Love is free. There is no payment required or needed. He does not owe you, nor should you want him to. Your deposits into the niceness, caring, doing-for-you bank account do not render him indebted. You can monitor someone's phone, check his emails, and hire a private investigator to keep tabs on him if you so choose. You can work your charm, get tough, make rules, and even berate him into submission. Perhaps he will have sex with you, and maybe you can even secure a relationship, marriage, and kids. However, you cannot, *make* someone want you the way that you want them to want you.

This is a non-negotiable point. His desire and commitment are either there, or they aren't.

Unfortunately, love can't be man-made. It's built on chemistry, and there's no rhyme or reason to chemistry. We can't purchase a bottle of Chosen Girl Spark Spray and, with it, manufacture a man who will love and desire us. If we could, we'd be with the guys we wanted back in high school. Hey, why stop there? If we could create things simply because we wanted them, we'd also be lunching with Spanx's creator, Sarah Blakely, at billionaire brunches in St. Tropez, dancing on piles of cash. Alas, that wasn't our path.

Don't you want to know whether someone would move a mountain for you of his own free will? Or, in some cases, simply lift his iPhone 13 Pro Max to his head to call you? (Or at the very least, ask Siri to do it?)

While we know it's hard to accept, he is yours if—and only if—he wants to be yours. We don't even like the word "yours" because it alludes to property, and people are not property. It's all about free-dom—about allowing a man to be as free as a butterfly, free to go at any time. This goes for you too—freedom is for all. It's such a beautiful concept, isn't it?

Yeah, right!

We admit that this is one of the more challenging lessons. A guy's ability to be free at any cost sounds fantastic and easy, in theory. You consider yourself a magnanimous, kind, fair woman, so why wouldn't you want him to be free? Hopefully, he lets you be who you are, and of course, you will extend the same courtesy to him. If he doesn't, that is a whole other conversation. For now, we are talking about you.

What *does* it mean to allow him to be free at any cost? It means that he is completely free to spend time with whomever he wants at any point in time. It means that he can do what he wants, be who he is, and live his life the way *he* wants to live it. If you want to know if he is truly yours, you will have to let him come to you of his own free will.

Most of us agree with this concept. We want him to be with us because he chooses to do so. But we like some safeguards, much like the alley guards for toddlers at the bowling alley. We may not realize that we are trying to control his friendships, excursions, and interactions by being passive-aggressive, overtly aggressive with ultimatums, or silently scorning. In our minds, we are subtly reminding him of the optimum behavior in a relationship.

But that's not even why we *really* do it. Every attempt to make him change or act a certain way for us to feel momentarily okay is based on fear. We are uneasy and need to feel better because we don't want to think about an outcome we don't want. Fear can come in many different forms. This particular doozy is the need to control, and trust us, it's every man's least favorite.

You may be panicking right now, looking back on a relationship and realizing that you manipulated and orchestrated everything from splitting the appetizer on date one to combining your families for the holiday season. Don't worry! All you have to do is loosen up your grip. See how he really feels by watching what he *does*. Actions tell us everything we need to know. We can see how important we are to someone and how much of a priority we are. But one vital detail to detect is does he *want* to be in a relationship? We see many things clearly once we're willing to let go, including whether or not a guy truly *wants* to be there.

Many dating rulebooks will tell you never to ask your man if he wants to commit. We'll talk about this further in a bit, but for now, the issue isn't about asking, "So, are we dating or in a committed monogamous relationship? Where is this going? Why haven't you changed your Facebook status?" We must let go of our need to know through words or the laying out of cookie crumbs, hoping he mindlessly follows the yellow brick road we have consciously (or unconsciously) curated.

It's time to open your eyes. Are you trying to turn snow into sunbeams? Before you decide whether or not you will let this man be a free butterfly, you need to know if he wants to be with you in the first place. Maybe he's only resting on the palm of your hand to take a bit of a break.

We are not looking for someone to simply be comfortable! We are looking for something epic. Right?

Jacqueline's Story

This principle is a doozy for me. I love focusing on every single need a boyfriend has, whether he expresses a need for my help or not. Starting a new business? No problem, let me build your website. Are you looking for an editor? I can hit up the contact I was saving for myself somewhere down the line (because you're more critical). I won't even get into how I played Florence Nightingale to my terminally ill boyfriend for three years yet. We'll explore that more later. Let's talk about that daytime soap actor instead—the one who used me as his personal therapist, unpacking and verbally vomiting all his woes about his flailing career and ex-baby-mamas. His male ego needed constant fluffing, mainly because his career was fleeting faster than my senses. I was his cheerleader, his safety line, his mind reader, and his chef. I was indispensable—basically, an assistant he was screwing—until I *was* dispensable, that is.

I learned that waiting in the wings to help instead of letting a butterfly soar on its own doesn't pay the bills, nor does it secure monogamy or love.

CHAPTER EIGHT

IT'S NOT PERSONAL
(DON'T TAKE IT THAT WAY)

Here's a little insider prostitute information (we're clearly diving right on into this principle). Note: We're not sure what the current appropriate term is for prostitute. Don't cancel us; we can assure you we are coming from a place of love. Okay, this may not officially *all* be prostitute insider info, but this insight did indeed come from prostitutes. Why does that matter? Because a prostitute is objective, transactional. She's not looking to get anything from the guy other than the cash left on the table. A prostitute can see clearly. She has no skin in the game (well, she does, but it's a different kind of skin). She's uninterested in what the relationship could or should be. Her assessment is based on pure, unbiased, harsh facts. Granted, seeing men in this element may sour her taste for them overall, but her perspective still provides exceptionally beneficial information.

One thing she knows for sure is that guys gravitate to the girls they are attracted to, no matter what. Let's imagine you have a line-up of girls, all equally beautiful. One is the "girl next door," one's a vixen, one's curvaceous, and one's exotic. They're all gorgeous, all fit, all equally desirable. A guy walks into a room, scans his choices, and his eyes light up for the vixen. Off they go.

(Please note that this is a simplified, on-the-nose example meant to give you a visual. Just roll with it.)

Another guy walks into the room and starts salivating for the exotic girl. In fact, he doesn't even notice the others, even though they are Jessica Alba and Claudia Schiffer doppelgängers. Off they go. Then another man walks in, and he too likes the vixen (she's back), and they leave. At some point, a man arrives who is solely interested in "girl next door" or curvaceous women. One day, the "girl next door" could rake in cash with a slew of men reliving their old Pamela Anderson *Baywatch* fantasies, and the next, she'd have no takers and go home with an empty Prada.

These women are confident, stoic, and secure. While we are *sure* there are insecure prostitutes out there, for the sake of this example, we are going to continue telling it the same way our informants shared it with us. They knew that men liked them or not and that it was not *ever* personal. Sometimes they were chosen; sometimes they were not. Sometimes, men would fall over them to catch a better glance at someone standing behind them, and sometimes they were on them like rabid dogs. Just as you are attracted to some men and not others, men are similarly attracted to certain women.

We certainly aren't suggesting that all guys have a precise type from which they never depart, but many do. There are always equal opportunists out there, but regardless, a man likes who he likes. Some men love rail-thin, skinny girls, and others like girls with a little meat on their bones. Still others like younger or older, taller, or shorter. There needs to be that spark, the je ne sais quoi, the undefinable glimmer. We've all felt it, but it runs deep in men. It goes well beyond having a "type," and it is never personal.

One more time for good measure: The moral of the story? IT'S NOT PERSONAL!

Is this realization as freeing for you as it was for us? Your efforts to be loved, adored, and desired by all men—or even that one man you really, really want—are a colossal waste of time. And further, your perfect hair, body, nails, eyelashes, and clothes won't change this!

Do you have any idea how much money we could have saved had we accepted this fact sooner? We remember a celebrity (we won't say her name because we adore her and don't want to shame her) who had the costs of her beauty regiment tallied one year to the tune of $300,000. We are not all receiving $2,500 monthly diamond microdermabrasion, so the annual total will be significantly less for us than it was for her. But it cost us a relative fortune, nonetheless. We are the first to say everything is perfect and a lesson, but damn, we wish we had done that African safari instead!

This does not mean you should move into a pair of sweatpants and stop working out. Men are also visual. We realize this is a sweeping generalization, but we absolutely do support you keeping up whatever fashionista, Manolo-wearing, Birkenstock chick, six-pack ab maintaining, surf casual, beach hair, coiffed hair, leisure wearing, manicured, gelled self you desire. But whatever regimen you adhere to, do it for YOU!

New goal: Be yourself! Instead of trying to be a master contortionist, spend time finding out what *you* like and stop trying to please him. Whether or not "Mr. X" likes you has nothing to do with your haircut, and if it does, you want to quickly kick him to the curb! Instead, be yourself with grace and dignity—because you will either be his type or you won't. You either float his boat, or you do not.

Did you hear music playing? We did.

To us, this information was the holy grail permitting us to simply STOP! He likes us, or he doesn't. There was nothing to do.

Now, do your best to not sit around on the couch eating HoHos all day, gaining weight by the kilo. The goal is to switch from trying to please *him* to trying to please *yourself*. There is nothing wrong with trying to be and look your absolute best. There is nothing wrong with looking beautiful and healthy—in your eyes and for YOU. But the idea that, somehow, what you look like will snag *and* keep a man is absurd. Trying to "look" a certain way to get a man will either never work, or it will backfire. So, you can let go of feeling hurt, rejected, or not enough if someone doesn't ask you out or looks away when you meet their gaze across the crowded bar.

We implore you to save your money and time trying to figure out how to get what you want. Get in shape, lose weight, take care of your skin, and wear sexy outfits for you and you only, but only do these things if YOU want to!

If you spend time investing in yourself, you will feel better about yourself. And this, dear friend, is the secret elixir that companies only wish they could sell. This is what is desirable to a man: a woman who is on fire in love with herself.

The confidence of not caring who finds you pretty, beautiful, or sexy is hot AF. It has nothing to do with the ominous "him" and only with how you feel about yourself. You have the power to feel good about who you are, and when you feel good about who you are, it doesn't matter what "he" thinks anyway!

Thinking that if we can capture what another woman possesses, he will turn his attention from her to us is an exercise in futility. It is a fight that will deplete you to your core. And we want you to learn to light up your core so that the right guy can see it. But the trick is lightning up your core for the sake of lighting up your core—NOT to get the attention of someone else.

You can now stop trying to get the attention of a guy who doesn't notice you. If he sees you, he will truly see you, and there is nothing you will be able to do to stop it. A little makeup or a new skirt won't matter. All the endless hours lost focusing on hurt feelings and comparison will disappear. It was never personal, and you couldn't have done anything to change what he thought after all.

Jacqueline's Story

There is always a way to "win" the man, I thought. I could simply change my looks. That's what I told myself. I finally got down to what I thought was a perfect and irresistible weight after breaking up with Steven. I then moved on to a Latin man whose ideal woman was Sofia Vergara. I had finally reached the most revered, worshipped body there was—or so I thought—waif-thin, 5'10, and 135 pounds. I finally looked like the women I had taped to my walls growing up. He hated it; his nickname for me was "bones."

My next "one" subtly threw jabs at my heels, big curly hair, and tight jeans, saying I was too "New Jersey" (whatever that means). I'd always prided myself on my crazy locks and 1980s outfits. Still, when he didn't like it, I became the J-Crew ad (which was what he thought was sexy) with my hair parted down the middle and straightened, wearing skinny jeans, white Keds, a flannel shirt, and no makeup. He loved it, and I stayed looking nothing like myself for the next six months.

I could continue to list examples of my real-life Julia Roberts role in *Runaway Bride*—changing who I was for every relationship. But no matter who I became, they still did what they wanted to do.

Also, if he asks you to change, he's probably not your guy. Just a hunch.

CHAPTER NINE

YOU CANNOT LOSE WHAT'S YOURS

B reak-ups are brutal. It can feel like your heart has been ripped right out of your chest. You would rather go to bed and wake up with an exposed root under a broken tooth with pain that ripples through you like lightning when touched than feel that way. If you've never been destroyed by love, you probably can't understand this feeling, but if you have, you know.

Nothing can save you from, alleviate, or heal this pain except some hope, a BFF you can relay *all* the details to from start to finish (over and over and over again), and maybe a few pints of (vegan) ice-cream. We have all suffered through those brutal break-ups. You know, the ones that leave you in a fetal position, screaming to God that if He brings him back, you'll work for the Peace Corps on every holiday for the rest of your life. This kind of pain guts you to a level you didn't even know existed. We have all had The One, or perhaps The Several, who made it painfully clear that there is no justice in the world. He will always be remembered as The One Who Got Away or The Guy Who Left, and no amount of praying, begging, or manipulating could get him back. He was The One who caused us to gain twenty pounds, lose twenty pounds, or become an insomniac. The One who, to everyone else, was a mildly attractive bar manager but to *you* was a guy who looked like George Clooney and had the money of Warren Buffet and the excitement of Mario Andretti.

But here's the thing…

You don't want to be with someone who doesn't want to be there fully and completely. And if you keep going back to the one you want to be The One, and he is not right for you, you won't be available for the guy who is!

We will now present you with the most infuriating question ever uttered: What are you willing to let go of to get what you want?! (More on this in chapter 14, Protect The King's Throne.) Let's say you are happy with booty calls and seeing him every now and then. Do you have to give that up?

If you want to, don't! Remember, we are not here to tell you what to do. We are only asking you to consider two things before (or after) you move ahead with this "after business hours only" adventure:

If he has already left and is not currently in your life, perhaps LET HIM GO and see if he returns.

And...

If he is a half-assed, scraps-giving guy you want more from, perhaps also let him go.

We are not soothsayers. He *could* completely change or tell you he will do anything to get you back (even though we've been doing this work for two decades, and we very much know it's hard to change even when you want to). He might ultimately propose, marry you, and live happily ever after with you! But how will you know if you never let go?

Jacqueline's Story

But what if *you* know he's yours, but he doesn't...yet?

That was the story I told myself when any man ran for the hills. There is one who stands out: Ed. I ended up with Ed immediately after breaking up with my live-in boyfriend of three years. Ed was quickly smitten with me. Gradually, after his many attempts at convincing me, the feeling became mutual. Six months in, his infatuation with me ended.

My investment in Ed was immense. I overlooked a bunch of my "no-ways," including two full tattoo sleeves, history as a cheater, and someone with whom I could not have a conversation about anything other than our "relationship." Regardless, I knew he was my guy and attempted every tactic I could to keep him, including befriending his mother and friends, writing his website, and even convincing him to give me sperm for my frozen eggs. I would NOT let go.

After six months of attempts, he drew a line in the sand. He asked me, only half-joking, if the only way I would let this go was if he left the state. He tried one more time to explain that we were not meant to be, embryos and all. While I fought tooth and nail to keep someone who wasn't mine, thank God he fought harder to leave.

In the past, I beat myself up for wasting time and not seeing the signs when they were presented. But I'm grateful that I went to such dedicated lengths to "get the guy." I now know that it doesn't work; you don't have to win over someone who is meant for you.

Oh, soulmate, where art thou?

Let's discuss the guy who is frequently nowhere to be found. This scenario can be complicated. Obviously, no situation is the same, and we all have different perceptions of relationships. It's easy to think, *Maybe this one is different? He's wounded from that girl in high school who broke his heart, and it has been wreaking havoc on any woman in his path since. He just needs to go slowly because he has commitment issues, but he knows it's different with me.*

We read into his messages, texts, and emails to grasp any words he says that support our case and the result we crave, even when his actions don't match his words (or his other actions). When his words and actions matched in the beginning and then suddenly changed, we stayed in denial of what was happening and focused on what was—or, even worse, what could be. Holding on to someone's potential or your carefully constructed fantasy of who they are can take years from your life. However, if you are willing to sit through the time of not having him, certain lessons are learned.

We know how much you want this guy to be your one and only. And if you know deep down that he really *is* right, can you walk through the pain of not having him to see whether he is The One? Can you tell yourself:

1) If he comes back to me, he is choosing to come back to me. I can choose to only want people in my life who are there because they have the freedom to be there.

2) If he isn't The One and doesn't come back, that means someone else is *way* better for me.

3) If I cannot lose what is mine, then holding on to any guy is a waste of energy. Why hold onto someone when I can't lose what is truly mine in the first place?

If he isn't for you, we promise (and we don't make many of those) that one day you will look back and thank God you took a leap of faith and let him go.

But we all want to keep our king's throne open (more on this concept later), and we, therefore, know you are going to obsessively ponder the following loop:

How many times have you asked yourself those questions? How many cell phone minutes have been spent assessing whether or not he would be sorry? How many books have we all read about properly behaving during the relationship or during the break-up to ensure he was left wanting us? We have all wanted to take a hostage instead of letting the process unfold naturally. Ultimately, hostage-taking never works.

Ask the questions. Cry it out. Go get that eighteenth psychic reading where you know you'll be told that he's your soulmate, but he's just shy. Buy the pendulum and swing away for your answer! Do whatever makes you feel better while you wait—without interfering—to see what he does.

Loop away. Wear out your best friend. Eat that ice cream. But somehow, in the deep vastness that is you, find a teeny, tiny smidge of hope that resonates with the truth that you cannot lose what is yours. If that doesn't hold, try this one on for size: If you can let him go without "help" on your part, you will see what he truly wants to do.

Help, in this instance, is exemplified by:

- An "accidental" text
- An "accidental" butt dial
- Sending a LinkedIn invitation
- Liking his Instagram or TikTok post
- Making a café down the road from his work your new office

"Help" is doing anything to remind him that you exist.

"But what if he forgets about me?" you ask. If he can forget you, HE ISN'T YOURS!

If he isn't your guy, we promise you that, eventually, you won't care. You read that right: *You won't care!* Even though it seems an impossible thought when you are in the thick of it, once you don't care anymore, you really won't. Time will pass, and heartbreak will fade. The fantasy of what you think was supposed to be keeps you hooked into the "him" of the moment. Both of us have believed that drug addicts, thieves, gay men, and criminals were The One. We were committed to the idea with all the evidence in the world pointing to the contrary—combined with the fact that he possibly outright said he didn't want to be there—made no difference.

Once you are willing to let go of the guy you think you want, your self-confidence and power will appear shockingly faster than you expect. Then the day will come when you'll meet another guy, and the old Mr. Wrong will call you to get together. That's nice, but you'll be busy. And while that day will almost certainly come (except in rare cases), it doesn't come when you are looking for it. It comes when you are over it. Eventually, if he isn't yours, you won't care. If he is, you'll know it.

Sara's Story

I'm not saying they all come back, but often, once you let go, they do (which can be so amusing when you no longer care). This is precisely what happened to me. The guy who led me to understand many of my lessons (the one I thought I would die without) came back. And he did so in an extremely dramatic fashion. It felt almost like a movie. But not a romantic comedy

—more of a Science Fiction flick. I couldn't believe it. He literally chased me down the street after I left a restaurant near my apartment with a friend. He was begging and pleading for me to come back while passionately exclaiming that he loves me. Um, what? This was the same guy I would have paid a million dollars to hear say he just liked me a lot while we were dating. If I still cared about him at all, it would have been the best day of my life, but I no longer did. Apparently, the universe zigged when I wanted it to zag, and it worked out as it should have. As our girl Alanis sings, "Isn't It Ironic. Don't you think?" If I had *wanted* him to come back, on the other hand, this scene could have been fodder for the next blockbuster rom-com. Because, in the end, you cannot lose what's yours.

P.S. In the final edit before publication I got an IG DM from him asking me to dinner. Ummm…we ended twenty-one years ago. But every year or two he touches base to check my availability and marriage status.

CHAPTER TEN

BEING NICE DOESN'T MATTER

It's the most common line uttered during the post-mortem break-up conversation: "I was so NICE!" In fact, if we had a dollar for every time we heard a woman say some version of this, we could buy a Stella bag. One each. And those bags are expensive.

We know you're nice. We know you're amazing. We know how generous and loving and kind and thoughtful you've been. We agree that working to put him through medical school and then giving up your career so he could be the doctor he always wanted to be was nice. We know that running his errands, doing his laundry, and cooking dinner every night for a decade was admirable. His ex was nasty. She didn't do anything for him, but you did. You listened, supported, and uplifted him non-stop. You sent him groceries and meals via Postmates because he was sick. You flew him to Vegas because he didn't have the money. You drove to him ninety percent of the time because he had to be at home.

Yes, you are *so* nice. Thank God you did all that you did. Thank God you gave up half your life, your dreams, and your time to truly show him how supportive and strong you were for him. We are not being sarcastic or passive-aggressive with these statements. We are genuinely so glad you went out of your way to be the best person imaginable for him. Why are we glad? Because now you can see that being (fill in the blank) doesn't mean shit.

Unfortunately, being too nice in love doesn't score you points. It may help you get an upgrade to business class or a second round of breadsticks, but it won't make someone love you. You will not hear him declare how perfectly his girl ironed his tie over drinks with his co-workers after work. Nope. Sorry. Just because you lent him a hand does not mean he will take yours. AKA, you cannot buy security and loyalty in love. We don't want to be redundant, so, if necessary, revisit chapter 7, "Let Him Be Free as a Butterfly," for a refresher. In short, you cannot do things to *get* things. He may feel obligated for a while, but eventually, he will do what he wants to do.

This doesn't mean you should become a nasty bitch. A very wise therapist once said, "It doesn't matter how beautiful a woman is. If she talks down to, disrespects or punishes her man long enough, he

WILL leave." That is also true.

We know this is getting confusing, and you may be wondering, *What kind of tightrope do I need to walk? I can't be nasty, and I shouldn't be nice. SO, WHO THE HELL SHOULD I BE?*

Here's the answer: Be whoever you are—a powerful woman who is doing YOUR life for YOU while letting him be him. He can also buy groceries. He can order his own food. He can also cook dinner a few nights a week. He can get a job to pay for his own school expenses. He can call an Uber. He can remember (or not) to call his mom for her birthday.

We are NOT suggesting that you avoid doing thoughtful things or helping him out. But take note if you are doing "nice" things to create your own feelings of securing and safeguarding the relationship. Are you doing it to be indispensable in his life and to establish a deep and necessary hold he can't let go of? Maybe you're afraid that he wouldn't be there if you didn't do all of it. If this is the case, it requires some soul searching, and it is a harsh truth both to admit and examine. It's probably going to make you uncomfortable. But won't it be more painful to look back in twenty years and say, "I wasted my life doing EVERYTHING for him"?

Here's the thing. You are not his mother. That's good news because he most definitely doesn't want to sleep with his mother. Trying to buy him stuff or create his business so that he can't leave will not make him love you. He won't owe you. And even if he does stay for a little while because of guilt or obligation, do you really want that?

It is vital that when you do something for someone, including your guy, you do it without expectation of anything. When he drones on and on about how hard it is for him to construct a letter to the chairman that would take you two seconds to whip up, you might say, "I know you will figure it out, honey." Believe it or not, men want to handle their own business. This certainly doesn't mean that he doesn't enjoy thoughtful actions (we know your loophole ways). We are talking about the things you do to keep him, overcompensating for that voice inside you that might be on to something.

This does not mean you need to change everything and never wash a dish if he used it. We are asking you to dig deep and see whether he wanted to be there with you and eat off your pretty china—or did you orchestrate the entire meal.

You already are amazing without having to become the modern-day Martha Stewart/Betty Crocker/Florence Nightingale! Live your life, and make sure he knows that he has complete freedom to come or go. He can take care of himself. You can take care of yourself.

Sara's Story

I have spent a lifetime trying to de-nice myself. My role in life was "the nice girl." My grandmother's motto was "It's nice to be nice." This philosophy was in my blood, and it bled into all areas of my life, including love. It was not something I wished away either. It took years of healing and therapy to eradicate it from my life. My first impulse is to put another person at ease first, myself second. It's an overwhelming urge to make another feel loved or heard or cared for.

Once I see myself doing this, I stop in my tracks and ask, "What do I want?" Or "Is this for them or me?" If I determine that action was for them and not myself, I must fight my own impulse and either shut my mouth and not offer to help or speak up if something doesn't feel right. Of course, I do this imperfectly all the time. It is hard to turn around a quality that makes up the essence of who you are as a person.

Us, then them.

CHAPTER ELEVEN

KNOW YOUR LOOPHOLES

S peaking of loopholes (since we alluded to them in the previous chapter), behind every red-flag-laden dream guy is a highly sought-after loop-hole. Prove us wrong. You know you have a case for one hiding up your sleeve. We see it. How are we reading into your soul again? Because we have also been there!

For the record, we love the thought of a good ol' loophole. It's like alien sightings; many are documented, and we're pretty sure they exist, but they're damn rare. And as hard as we look, we rarely see them.

We know...

- Your cousin's sister reformed a "player" with one kiss.
- Your friend from college dated a married

man, and he left his wife for her.

- Your co-worker got married after one week of dating, and that was thirty years ago.
- Your boss's best friend had sex on the first date, and they are still in love.
- Your neighbor's aunt turned her lying, cheating husband into a monogamous yogi.

And the biggest loophole of all: Amal tamed George Clooney!

Your loophole, AKA "it will happen for me, because it worked for my aunt in 1984" is like a free pass for your own bullshit. Meaning, it will distract you from what is really happening.

We are not saying these miracles didn't happen. We love a great success story as much as the next girl. And by the time this book comes out, maybe we will finally be able to add some "real-life" examples. We just can't seem to think of any…yet. *But they are real*. And so are aliens. (We are not being sarcastic.)

Let's genuinely celebrate all loopholes. We really are rooting that your guy is The One. With that said, we want to stress something: Loopholes can derail you. Loophole thoughts will slide in like a stealth fighter jet, fast and furious. You won't even realize it's a loophole-kind-of-thought right away (or ever). It might even be undetected completely and hide under the guise of "This situation is different. He's different."

But is he?

If you have taken our words to heart and applied our suggestion to let him go to see what he does, and he is *not* coming back without your "help," how different is he? Perhaps he isn't available. Or he's made it clear that you are not at the forefront of his mind. If so, why is he an exception?

Because you *want* him to be, that's why. We have already said this numerous times: You want him to be The One. You know our ideas are great in theory, or they are perfect words to give to someone else, but when you only want his face, his voice, his smell—specifically his—you aren't yet ready to risk seeing the truth. But you will be. If you try these principles on for size, you will ultimately know where he stands, with or without the loophole.

We aren't asking you *not* to believe in loopholes or laugh at them or treat them like conspiracy theories. We want you to believe and hope, but while you do, open your eyes to see who he is and whether or not he sees you in the same way.

No one said this was easy.

CHAPTER TWELVE

THROUGH SICKNESS AND HEALTH, THOU SHALT REMEMBER...

You hear stories all the time about a wife standing by her husband's side for his entire professional career. Then something tragic happens—he gets sick or has an accident, and she sticks with him through it all, lovingly nursing him back to health. A miracle happens, he recovers, and then, as if by magic, he leaves his wife for his young nurse or new assistant.

We are not saying that a man *will* cheat and leave his wife if he gets sick, but we *are* saying that an individual met with a life-or-death challenge *can* cheat and leave his wife. Why? Because he is human, and why the hell not? A man is still *that same man*, whether he is sick or healthy. Please note that we are not uttering the ever-so-popular phrase "A man is a man" because that is a generalization. We are saying that if a man is a cheater, he will cheat—no matter the circumstances. It's a subtle but critical difference in semantics. This also applies to women. Cheaters will cheat.

We construct stories in our heads. If he's sick, and I am there for him 24/7, he will appreciate me. If he is poor, he will adore me more. His perceived imperfections or "baggage" give us an illusion of safety.

Dating a poor guy because you think he will be less likely to cheat rarely works, and rock stars can be faithful. Both can be true. What's important to note is that the successful, faithful rock star is also an inherently faithful person!

Sickness is not an exemption. No one knows this more than Jacqueline.

Jacqueline's Story

Mitch was the perfect love story, the one your best friend tells at your wedding. Had we gotten to that point, I imagine that the story would have gone something like this:

"Jacqueline, the woman who searched near and far for her 'One,' knew him all along. Her college boyfriend reemerged at the perfect time, and it was instantaneous love once again. They were together and knew that they were to be life partners. It was also a tragic love story, of course. Mitch had a terminal illness that was progressing with age, and he only had another ten to fifteen years to live. But, as we all know, love conquers all, and Jacqueline and Mitch were in it until death do they part."

And I was. I was there with him through it all. His mother's and father's deaths, his hospital stays, countless sleepless nights of him coughing and vomiting until 6:00 am when he finally passed out from exhaustion. Mitch had a brutal, cruel disease with a death sentence, and he wasn't supposed to live past the age of twenty-five.

His illness was accompanied by excruciating pain, hamstringing the way of life and activities he loved. As an ex-athlete and tougher-than-nails stubborn son of a bitch, he never complained. There was not a victim bone in his body. I took the brunt of his discomfort. I was the closest person in the world to him and, as such, the recipient of every ounce of his frustration, anger, pain, and sadness. I tried everything to make him feel better. I cleaned, cooked, and planned for us because he didn't have the energy to do so most of the time.

So yes, because he was sick, I overlooked every single dating ebb and flow and male/ female energetic back-and-forth we speak of in this book. They didn't exist. He was sick, and I believed that trumped everything I had learned.

The misery he experienced was accompanied by all-encompassing, unconditional love. Regardless of how much he pushed me away, scared to show his vulnerability and fear about mortality, I stood firm. I would love him no matter what. And he loved me to the extent that he could. I sat by his bed, three years after we reconvened, holding his hand as he lay in a coma. Ten days straight, all day, alone with him, until I could finally be there when he was taken off life support. Was it tragic? Yes. But did I know I loved him despite his illness and his reactions? Yes. This was Romeo and Juliet in modern-day life.

I was going to make his life count. Not even an hour after he died, I planned to create a foundation in his name and outlined the screenplay of our life in my mind. Without a full day of grief under my belt, I woke up to a sudden plot twist, one that wasn't in my storyline.

Apparently, Romeo liked to screw prostitutes on the side.

I never had a reason to doubt him. So when he gave me his passwords to everything on date five, my trust only was solidified. But when I was left with his belongings while organizing his bags, I couldn't help but notice the Erotic Review website's notifications. Apparently, he had been sleeping with and "Yelp" reviewing prostitutes in the most degrading and misogynistic ways possible for the past fifteen years. While he didn't have the strength or the inclination to plan a holiday for us, he sure as shit could organize clandestine paid meetings with a twenty-two-year-old. It didn't matter how nice, loving, kind, open, sensitive, attentive, and different I was. His loyalty to us was compartmentalized. He would act out his imminent mortality and loss of control however he wanted. I rationalized that maybe the guilt made him lash out. Perhaps it was the physical pain.

But then I was reminded that he is a man, and while this doesn't mean that all men (sick or not) sleep with prostitutes, it meant that *this* man did. And because he was sick, I overlooked who he was because of the circumstances. The signs were there if I looked past his disease. I would never have guessed his hobby, but the way he reviewed those prostitutes was the way he talked to me. The safety net of a man acting a certain way because he was terminally ill was a mere illusion. There are no safety nets. People are who they are, and no matter who I am or how I act, that fact is unchangeable.

In the end, a man is faithful *because he is a trustworthy person.* He is not faithful because he makes less money than you, has extra weight on him, or rents a crappy apartment on the wrong side of town. Neither jobs, status, health, nor looks influence his moral compass. You will *not* be treated differently because you deem a particular characteristic of their life "worse" than yours. The key is to see him for who he is.

CHAPTER THIRTEEN

CONSIDER CATS AND DOGS (AND DOLPHINS)

To suggest that girls are like cats and guys are like dogs is cliché, we know. But the most banal platitudes generally prove true over time, and cliché or not, that particular one is exceptionally suited for this chapter.

We stoically stand behind a fully empowered woman being capable of manifesting whatever she wants. So yes, we are feminists by that definition. But we don't believe men and women should be approached in the same way when it comes to matters of the heart. Before you throw this book at your air fryer, hear us out.

Men are men. Women are women. We know you've read *Men Are from Mars, Women Are from Venus*, and if you haven't, absolutely do. We can't attempt to out-do that message (nor do we need or want to), but we can break it down in a different way. Keep in mind, we don't believe in sweeping generalizations, but for the sake of this chapter, we are going to put some forth.

Maybe you'll understand the concept a bit better if we use the language of house pets. Obviously, women are the cats. Women, like cats, pounce and stride with a queen's pride. They love to be praised and adored and told they're beautiful. When abused or mistreated, they cower and lack trust, often hiding from the world. Only a truly loving person can heal them, finally coaxing them out from hiding to be loved once again. Hint, hint…you need to love yourself first.

Men, on the other hand, are dogs. Usually, that phrase is meant to be derogatory, insinuating that men want to hump people's legs all the time. We won't talk about that here (though we're sure humping legs is enjoyable). Instead, we are referring to men as dogs when it comes to their aim to please and their ability to focus on one thing at a time. When they are abused, they can be lovingly coaxed out of hiding simply with love and food.

Cats are complicated. Dogs are simple and straightforward.

Again, this is a very dumbed-down example. We can go into specific cases of males you know who are cats and females who are more dog-esque. For instance, Jacqueline is totally like a dog, and Sara is like a cat. STILL, FORGET ALL THAT! We are not going to dive into that loophole. Our case has nothing to do with that.

We present you with...

Exhibit A: The Litter Box

What happens when you rescue a feral cat that has never been indoors? (Allow us to use this opportunity to give a little plug for rescuing cats.) What about a newborn kitten? How do you teach them to go to the bathroom in the litter box? We know that the doling out of treats you do with your poodle will not work for these aloof, skulking queens. Instead, you put the litter box in the middle of the room, and they will go right there. They'll gravitate toward it—cats like taking a shit in sand. Go figure. We don't know why, and we will not offer a host of options for this mysterious and inexplicable behavior. Honestly, who the hell cares. All we know is: THEY JUST DO!

On the other hand, a dog would never, ever instinctively run to the plastic crate of sand to take a pee. A dog would need to be trained to go inside the house in a box. Dog owners leash up their pups and take them around the corner for a bathroom adventure. Let's go one step further. Just as cats love the sand, dogs love grass. And trees. And fire hydrants. And sidewalks if they live in New York City. Defecating outdoors is their jam.

Yes, outdoor cats also go outdoors. But in most cases, when indoors, they are looking for that sandy dirt (probably your Feng Shui Ficus in the corner) to do their thing.

What is the moral of this story? Cats love litter boxes. Dogs can be trained to go in a litter box. BUT...

1. It will be awkward.

2. It will probably embarrass the dog (and dogs hate to be shamed).

Why not let dogs free-ball it outside on their fun little excursions and let the cats sit in their goddess-like sun patches and tinkle when they are called to do so? You can make one do the other, sure, but why not amplify the true nature of each? Everyone and every animal thrives when they do what comes to them instinctively. However, if one day you find your dog squatting in a cat box or your cat with a leash in its mouth at the front door, you can celebrate the hell out of that too!

Exhibit B: Dogs, Cats, and Dolphins, Oh My!

The revelation that males are dogs and females are cats is old news, but it makes a great off-the-cuff comparison. Here's the thing, some people's love interest is more like a cat, but they want it to be a dog. Conversely, some people's love interest is like a dog, but they want it to be a cat. If you only knew the number of calls that we've received over this very issue (women barking orders at their men as if they were dogs because they really wanted cats), you'd refund us a couple of years on our birth certificates.

- I TOLD him I like to get calls on the hour, every hour…
- I TOLD him that I need to get flowers to feel appreciated…
- I AM SO LIVID that he didn't check in with me after work like I told him I need him to…
- I ASKED him not to go out with that friend…
- I TOLD him I like to talk about my day before he watches the news…
- I AM SO MAD, AND I TOLD HIM.
- HOW DARE HE _____ WHEN I TOLD HIM _____.

And on it goes—women angry that their dog is acting more like a cat and vice-versa.

If a guy does not fit what you want after kindly and respectfully letting him know what makes you feel safe and adored, perhaps he is not your guy. Like it or leave it. Something works for you, or it doesn't. Sometimes we complain about a dog when we really want a cat. And sometimes, we try (unsuccessfully) to turn a German Shepard into a mountain lion.

Let's say you love romantic walks on the Seine River in Paris with your monogamous lover, AKA French Bulldog (it was low-hanging fruit). You would be wasting your time trying to turn your polyamorous lover who doesn't believe in marriage into your exclusive romantic partner, just as you would trying to turn a Dalmatian into a dog without spots (this one landed on us). You would be barking (we can't stop) up the wrong tree. Meaning, stop trying to turn someone into someone he is not.

Jokes aside, stop trying to turn a dog into a cat because...

1. By their very nature, they hate being chastised

2. If you are trying to turn a dog into a cat, it won't work and you will exhaust yourself

You can speak your truth fully and completely. You can own what works for you and what doesn't. You can stand up for yourself and say what hurts. Be you, of course (we would never tell you not to be). But learn what confidently and respectfully expressing your needs and truth looks like. Guilting someone into bringing you flowers because your cheating ex made you feel unappreciated may get you a delivery or two. But one day, he will feel obligated and pressured, and 1-800-FLOWERS will not get a re-dial.

Let's use the flowers example. If flower deliveries are a must for you and you aren't getting any after you told him that you needed them to feel seen, how do you handle it? How do you let him know what works and what does not?

We promised you a dolphin, so here it goes:

Men are a lot like dolphins. While we use and love the cat/dog analogy and agree with it, we believe men are more like dolphins than dogs.

This theory began in the early 1800s. We're kidding. It started in the early 2000s when Sara's spiritual healer would say, "Men are like dolphins. They thrive on praise and not punishment." She continued to explain that most women yell, belittle, or punish men into doing what they want, treating them, quite literally, like dogs. She argued that men really want to please. Therefore, if you want them to take out the trash because they are lagging, don't yell, "You lazy sod, take out the trash." Instead, say *(one time)*, "I love it so much when you help me with the trash." Or, if he were to do it on his own, praise him by saying, "Oh my God! I love it SO much when you take out the trash. You are the best ever." (Say it more in your words and less like a Valley Girl.)

Because dolphins love to be rewarded (and keep in mind, this information comes from Sea World, a place we never visit but will use for the sake of this example), they will continue to do whatever it was that was praise-worthy repeatedly. So do dogs. Another mind-blowing fact: Humans do too! I think we are on to something big here.

In general, humans do better with praise. What man on this planet has ever become perfect because you talked down to him? Can you think of any? Other than some random submissive you knew in college? Exactly.

Men "work" better when they are praised. For the most part, men want to make you happy. They love to make you happy. Maybe some men don't care if you are happy or not, but that is the biggest tell of all, isn't it?

We're sorry for being so straightforward, but men are not your servants. Although men intrinsically desire to please their mate, they are not here to be your bitch. We are here to love, unite, and make happy lives together. It's essential to stop when you find yourself yelling agendas, telling them who to be and how to do things to fit into your world. That goes in the "your issues, not his" category.

Instead of trying to get dogs to become cats and cats to become dogs, why not take this approach for a whirl: Let men thrive doing what they do best. You do what you do best, and you praise them for anything you deem praiseworthy. (You can even take that suggestion into your life in general. Remember, we get more of what we love.)

If you think we are too old-fashioned with this, be sure to read the final chapter. We are pushing freedom for self, which means freedom for others too. It means allowing men to be themselves. We can't change anyone except ourselves.

Jacqueline's Story

It's infuriating. I simply don't understand why men cannot follow simple directions. When my brother was getting married in Ireland, we planned to be there for two full weeks. It would be an incredible experience trekking up and down the coast with my boyfriend (the one battling a terminal illness) after the two-day extravaganza. It would be an epically romantic trip, holding hands and strolling through the land where *Game of Thrones* was filmed. Little did I know, our relationship would mirror *The Battle of the Bastards*.

Mitch had still not purchased his plane ticket, and every time I asked, he doubled down in defiance. As the event drew closer, my anxiety grew with each day he did not buy the flipping ticket. The more anxious I became, the more I tried different tactics to force him into booking a flight. I nagged; he rebelled. I put brochures about Ireland around the apartment; he ignored me. Finally, one day I was silently scorning him while he was watching a Patriots game, *not* plugging his credit card number into Delta. He looked up and said, "You do realize that the more you demand and order me to buy this ticket, the longer I will wait."

I realized that he was procrastinating to oppose my controlling (I like to color it organized, meticulous, and prompt) way of being. Finally, I surrendered to the fact that he wasn't going to come. The bottom line is, I let go of my need for him to do what I wanted. Four days later and the day before we were all to leave, he forwarded me his itinerary.

Sidenote: it was a red flag that he would purposely stress me out, leaving me wondering if I would have a plus one. I just didn't see it because he was sick.

PROTECT THE KING'S THRONE

What are you willing to let go of to get what you want?

When Sara first heard this question, she was sobbing over a guy she was sure was her soulmate (even though he wasn't aware of that fact). The person who said it was trying to point out something very simple: If he *isn't* your guy (and it wasn't looking good at this point) and you say you want a great relationship (even if you think you love this guy who is currently not in your life), you should clear the space for the great relationship that you say you want.

WHAT?! Even if I want *him* to be that great relationship, should I clear the space?

Yes.

This sounds like that Marie Kondo cleaning-out-your-closet theory. But isn't that only valid with sweaters, jeans, and old coats, not relationships you're messing around with simply to pass the time? No. This is a rule that transcends all aspects of life. If you want something to come into your life, you must clear out the clutter already taking up space.

Does this mean you have to go so far as to clear out a relationship you don't care about? Or any others you may be in? Yes. Which one? Both.

Whether you are madly in love with someone currently not in your life or you are filling time with a take-it-or-leave-it guy, you may want to empty that space for your *true* guy. You want a crazy, passionate, soul-igniting relationship, right? Then why not create a space for what we call the King's Throne. You get the picture. A king. On a throne. All regal and manly and shit. Ready to fight for you. So hot.

"But I want 'X' guy to be it. I don't want any other kings. I know the universe may have someone better, but I want *him*!" We really do hear you on that. But let us remind you of your new mission: to find a king that is worthy of you being his queen!

"But why can't I hang out with this one while I wait for the one I want?!" you wonder.

While we've engaged in many spiritual pursuits to "fix" our lives and make everything better, there was one truism that permeated every religion, philosophy, and teaching: Everything is energy. If we are all made up of energy and can influence—if not create—our own lives, is it not crucial to focus our energy where it needs to be? If you are dating someone and are acutely aware that he isn't your guy and you are passing the time with him, you may be blocking that perfect-for-you guy: your king!

Sara's Story

When I was going to my spiritual healer, seeking relief from heartbreak, all I wanted was for "him" to come back. It would have been so much easier if there had been a simple formula for that. I hated knowing that her words—"What are you willing to let go of in order to get what you want?"—were resonating as truth. Even though I wanted this guy to be The One, I knew deep down that I would have to walk through the pain of *not* having him to know if he was actually "The One." What she said was simple. Annoying but simple.

1. If he came back to me, he was choosing to come back to me, and I should only want people in my life who were there because they were free to be there (or not).

2. If he wasn't The One, that meant there was someone else out there who was better for me.

3. If I cannot lose what is mine, holding onto any guy is a waste of energy. Why hold onto someone when you can't lose what is truly yours in the first place?

During that heartbroken period, I worked on the goal of keeping my king's throne vacant and available. It was hard because my only concerns at that time in my life were:

Will he miss me?

Will he come back?

Will he know what he lost out on by losing me?

Will he regret it?

He did not come back. Well, he did much later, a moment I described at the end of chapter 9, and remember, by that point I had ceased to care. But knowing that he *could* was what kept me going for a while. Heartbreak is a bitch.

The king's throne is the energetic space that your Mr. Right will ultimately occupy, and your Mr. Right will be astounding. Yes, even better than that one you can't get over. Or who knows, it may even be him! But you won't know until you clear out the room. You must be free to let whomever that "him" is into your life.

Let's talk about placeholders for a moment. First, there's the booty call you think is funny but not a long-term relationship guy. If you *know* he isn't your future, then it's time to let him glide into your past. And, FYI, we place no judgment on nor have any issues with booty calls. Go for it and have fun. But as a good friend once said: "If you want a boyfriend, only date guys who WANT to be in a relationship."

If you want a *boyfriend*, clear the path so he can get to you. Create space for him to see you! If you are unavailable, an available guy (with integrity) won't see you. Like attracts like.

Second, let's chat about the placeholder guy, specifically, the one who buys you dinner and is always available when you need that "plus one." You are not interested in him long-term, but he's still there for you in a pinch. If you want to be with someone who is emotionally free and available, you must *be* emotionally free and available. If you are dating someone to "pass the time" or for the sake of convenience, you are not accessible. Instead, you have some dude occupying your king's throne. Get it?

And, for the record, free and available means he is single. He is interested in meeting someone. He is NOT living in his ex-wife's spare bedroom and only wanting a hook-up. He's free of complications versus complicated AF.

Jacqueline's Story

It's impossible to know who could have been my king in my late twenties. I could not take my focus off tracking Mark's every movement long enough to even notice another man in the room. I spent over 13,000 minutes a month discussing him with every friend or stranger, analyzing every conversation we had, and trying to throw other men in the mix during our "off" months. These other men included a US boxing champion, a lawyer, and a restaurant entrepreneur, but it would not have mattered if Brad Pitt himself swooped in; someone occupied my throne, and he took every bit of my mental energy.

I missed out on life experiences like trips to England, Idaho, the Catskills, and time spent with my family during the holidays because I was glued to the phone, waiting for the man I thought was my king to call. Spoiler alert: He was not a king; he was not even a frog. I can't cry today over guys I might have met in the past because that is a waste of energy. But I do know that you can't meet someone who can't get to you.

What if you haven't yet moved on to someone else, but you are still occupying all your time obsessing over the last guy—waiting for him to call and rehashing his horrible ways to your girlfriends? If you are doing this, you are still not clearing the room. You don't need to be sitting down to dinner with someone or be in his bed to be energetically blocking someone else.

When you remain stuck in the cyclone of "him" and trying to lure him back, you are prolonging your pain. We are *not* saying, "Don't grieve a relationship." If you are still heartbroken, you're probably not available for love anyway. Take time to heal and get over your ex. If he isn't coming back, or even if you are still in the hopeful phase, you will at some point feel everything you need to feel. There's no escaping it, and there is no rush. When you are ready, you can come back and toss your (energetic) cards on the table.

Sometimes, after grief, anger will surface. When that happens, the anger about your ex clogs up your king's throne with toxic energy. If you hang onto your self-righteousness, continuing to regurgitate all the ways he did you wrong, you may miss out on a chance at great love simply because you are not available.

How many times have you drifted through the day, caught up in your head (if not your phone), dissecting a relationship that is long over? How many conversations have we all had, asking our girlfriends what a certain text meant or why he hasn't called? We try to figure out the problems in a relationship we knew wasn't going anywhere. We know it's done. We know it's over, yet we loop it over and over. For all we know, we might be walking past our future husband at the grocery store and not even see him because we are energetically unavailable.

Isn't it time to get what you want? One, two, three...go time! Clear that shit out!

Sara's Story

This principle was hard for me. I really, *really* wanted to keep going back to an old relationship to fix it. I had to keep letting it go over and over again mentally and often say out loud: "If he is meant for me, he will come to me. But for now, I have to let him go." Then, I'd go back to my therapist and ask her again, "What was it you said? Tell me again." I needed to be continually reminded to let go.

She'd say, "Let go of the old to let in the new…clear out that king's throne so 'your' guy can see you.'"

"Oh yeah, right…got it."

Then, I'd talk to my friends and run over every detail a few more times. It's so difficult when we want what we want, and I *really* wanted this guy to be my king. Of course, he ended up not being The One, a reality for which I am now very grateful. Sometimes you can't see a situation clearly until it is a distant memory.

CHAPTER FIFTEEN

THE HOT DOG VERSUS THE STEAK

W e're vegan. Have we mentioned this yet? Yes, vegans love to tell everyone that they're vegan. We're telling you now (again) because this chapter title alone is awkward for us but calling it "The vegan hotdog and the cauliflower steak" was a little too wordy. We also want to be authentic to what we have touted for the past two decades, and that, my friend, is "The hot dog versus the steak." We would rather risk being un-cool and, in this case, meaty, than create something new for the sake of something more entertaining.

We recently heard the same sentiment in the phrase: "Focusing on a rhinestone when there's a diamond around the corner." This one is more modern, but whether it's a rhinestone, a hot dog, or a Morning Star corndog on a stick, the message is the same: Why settle when there is something better waiting for you?

If you do, you are accepting scraps, also known as a half-assed relationship that gives you just enough to keep you there. The experience can be best summed up by your best girlfriend's words while you're pining away for the cheating scumbag who broke your heart for two years even though he did bring you a small stuffed animal for your birthday: "Why are you settling for crumbs?"

Women don't do this with only their partners. How many times have you been devastated over something—a job, an apartment, a trip—not working out? The only thing you can see is that it didn't end up the way you wanted, but in hindsight, you also realized that it was not meant to work out that way. There was an alternative situation—a different job, a better home, or a more convenient flight—right around the bend. The same is true with relationships, but at the time, we myopically focus on "that one," and any deviation from our desired outcome seems insane.

We have seen this play out in our lives, over and over. We all have stories about how everything ultimately worked out better than expected, even though we were shattered at the time. We often don't want to admit it once we realize it. Also, we want him to be the steak! We want that for you too. But let's assume for a minute that we don't know where he falls on the hot dog/steak spectrum.

Let's talk about your *dream* guy, your dream relationship. This is the man who is good enough for you. This is not the one you are contorting yourself for, doing everything in your power to attract or keep, all because you don't feel good enough for *him*. Is he worthy of such a bad-ass, gorgeous, amazing woman such as yourself? Is he good enough for you!

Now that we are on the same page…

Your dream guy is not going to *let* you get away. He will not mess with fate. He will not want any other man to get you, have you, or win you. If he is your guy, you won't be able to beat him away with a stick. There will be nothing half-assed about it. He will *show* you that he feels this way. Yes, he will probably tell you, but words can be cheap, confusing, and open for interpretation. Action is the big-ticket item, and if he is *your* guy, he'll be on it.

Now, how do you let go of the juicy hot dog when you really want him to be the steak? It doesn't matter what your fancy-pants therapist says, how closely you follow "the rules," or how many Instagram posts you read about how to get him back. When you are done beating your head against the wall, you will finally see it. When you realize he is not the steak (and that he has been a hot dog all along), you will find freedom. With that freedom will come resolute confidence that if you let go of that mini dog in a bun, you will encounter someone better for you.

We can't see around corners. The man of your

dreams may very well be lurking at the mobile pick-up area at Starbucks in a couple of weeks. Remember, we can't expect to bring in something great if our energy is clogged up with a time-waster. We won't see Mr. Perfect if we are sniveling over someone we know is wrong, but we also don't like to be alone on Saturdays.

How do we know this? How can we summon the faith to believe something like this? Because we have seen it all before. And so have you. Remember that "dream" job you didn't get, but then the truly perfect one showed up a week later, and it's where you met your new BFF? How many times have you found yourself in those situations?

There is another crucial point to this rule: You don't want anything that isn't meant for you. It's hard to wait for the steak when you have that hot dog in front of you. But isn't it also exhausting trying to be satisfied by that hot dog? If we are dealing with a guy who is not meant to be with us, we can become triggered and use other tactics to ensure he stays. Perhaps we attempt to keep him interested by buying sexy lingerie or getting spray tans, acrylic nails, or longer eyelashes. Or maybe we try to energetically alter things by ignoring his calls, so he misses us or flirting with other men to keep him on his toes.

The game plan is intricate; there are many options. They have all been executed over and over again. However, what you'll find is that you'll always need to execute one more. The game will never end, and your efforts will never be enough to keep his eyes on the ball (you).

If you have to tightly clutch him, he isn't your guy. Let him go and let him flow, and if he comes back to stay of his own free will, then you can trust that this is something meant to be in your life.

On the other hand, if he does indeed go, move on to the next!

"WHAT?" you exclaim. "This isn't fair. I let go of the hot dog, and you promised me a steak. WTF? This is bullshit." Correct, we did, and it is. But sometimes you need to know what kind of steak you are dealing with to really, *really* know. And don't forget, a steak requires a little longer of a wait than a hot dog.

For this chapter's purpose, we assume that you really want "him" to be a steak, and if he stays in your life, you will be happy. If he vacates the premises, you will be really upset now, but you will later see that it was worth it. Either way, you'll know it's for your greater good. Your steak is coming. Trust the chef.

Bon Appetit.

Sara's Story

I have a friend who was being heavily pursued by a famous actor. Unfortunately, he was known for being quite a player. He wasn't hiding the fact that he didn't want to settle down or have an exclusive relationship with anyone. In fact, he was very clear it was going to be nothing more than a booty call. I asked her what she wanted, and she said she wanted a boyfriend.

Sometimes it's easier to walk away when the vision of something long-term doesn't seem terribly enticing. Many girls I know throw all their rules away when someone "famous" or "rich" or "really hot" presents himself. Even when they say they would never do that…they do.

In this case, the actor pursuing my friend was one of those desirable types. I told her that there was nothing wrong with hooking up with him and having a fling, but if she wanted a boyfriend (as *she* defined the concept of "boyfriend"), he wasn't going to be the one. She could choose to go there, but she would eventually have to let go of him to find her heart's desire (a true boyfriend). Sometimes, the longer you're in even an undesirable relationship, the harder it gets to leave.

In the end, she didn't hook up with the actor, which I'm sure was not easy. I was surprised because he was famous, rich, *and* hot. Talk about a test of faith—turning down one of the most eligible men on television. The most hilarious part of this story was what happened next (the universe has the best sense of humor). After she walked away, she met a movie star who actually wanted to be in a relationship. Shortly after that, they got married and had kids.

The moral of the story is not about trading one actor for another. It isn't about dating actors at all (not that we have any issues with that). It's about the importance of knowing what you want. My friend wanted a boyfriend, so she hung in there for someone who also wanted to be in a relationship. Period. The fact that he also happened to be a famous actor was a random "coincidence."

CHAPTER SIXTEEN

PAY ATTENTION TO PATTERNS

O PEN YOUR PEEPERS! Or, as a friend quoting her mom says, "Turn the volume down on the TV and watch the show."

We can save so much time by opening our eyes to what is right in front of us, but we generally don't take the time to look. We remain head in the sand, ostrich-like, denying any information that gets dropped in our laps.

Curious, isn't it? Because we like the "idea" of someone, we are willing to hypnotize ourselves out of reality. We create an alternative universe to fit our narrative, which prevents us from seeing the truth. Why do we do this? We are smart women. We did well in school, run several businesses simultaneously, create posts for our "brand," making sure our four million followers get fresh content every single day (and let's not forget our dog's page, too), are mastering Duolingo in Chinese and French, and can cook a five-course meal while filming every step of it. (Don't get us wrong, we're impressed.)

In short, we are consummate multi-taskers.

So why are we blinded by such straightforward facts? Very simple… because we want to be. This topic comes up so often during our random conversations with women seeking advice. The scenarios vary, but the solution remains the same: It is your job to be patient and collect information.

Everyone loathes this revelation. We all want to know, and we want to know *now*! However, all the answers to your questions can be found by opening your eyes. Pretend you're a private investigator or in the CIA. We know you would kick ass in those professions, given the way you can Google and fact-check a man's entire life. Admit it. You're stellar at it. You know who every single one of his Instagram followers is, how they met, and whether or not they are single. You are, at your core, an information getter, yet you choose not to see what is right in front of you. You are an intel-gathering truth seeker who is taking responsibility for what you see.

We would like to make this more fun—not fun like a Saturday afternoon in Sephora fun—but we invite you to change your perspective in this area. As Sara's therapist used to say, "You can't really know who someone is for at least a year." Sara scoffed at and rejected this notion at the time. Though we concur that a lot of information is revealed within a yearly calendar life cycle, there's a long stretch between casually half-absorbing that information and being a modern-day Nancy Drew. More importantly, we don't need an entire year to figure some of this stuff out.

In fact, we have continually found that you can determine who someone is on the very first date. You probably have most of the needed information before your appetizer even arrives—*if* you pay attention.

- Does he endlessly talk about himself as though he's more fascinating than Gandhi?
- Is he thoughtful about what *you* want?
- Does he ask you about your life?
- Does he remember what food you like? Or does he take you to a steak house after you told him you're a vegan?
- Does he glance around the room to check out other women?
- Does he make eye contact with you, or do his eyes dart around like a criminal nervous about his latest crime spree?
- Does he pick you up on time, or does he arrive forty-five minutes late without a phone call or an apology?
- Does he call you last-minute and expect you to immediately drop your laundry and

> run over to his place?
>
> - Does he say "Please" and "Thank You," or does he have the manners of a caveman?
> - Does he open the car door for you, or does he leave you hanging on the curb?

We are not judging the answers either way. It's simply important to *allow* someone to be who he is. You may get irate if a guy doesn't text you every morning to start the day, while another girl might find that level of attention grating. It's key to welcome who someone is, flaws and all. This way, we truly know if they're a match for us.

SIT BACK AND WATCH THE PATTERNS

This perspective shift is a game-changer. If we could only pick one section of this book for you to read and truly absorb, this would be it.

You must sit back and thoughtfully observe *who someone actually is.* How does he treat women? Respectfully? Like objects? Who are his friends? Are they nice? Kind? Compassionate? Does he take care of his responsibilities? Does he do what he says he'll do? Does he keep his commitments? Does he have addictions? Does he only want to see you at his place (or yours)? Does he have a job? Does he tend to call last-minute or only when you're not available?

If you can't identify a pattern by closely watching (although we suspect you can most of the time), a direct question works. Ask him how he feels about relationships. What does an ideal partnership look like to him?

Maya Angelou said, "When somebody shows you who they are believe them." Even though we observe who a person is, we rarely truly *see* them. People *always* tell us exactly who they are from the very beginning. If you could shave off two years of your precious time by listening to friends who heard a guy was a cheater, would you do so? Is saving yourself from potential heartache worth asking some uncomfortable questions? Remember, this lesson works both ways. There is always the possibility that everyone loves him and has nothing but positive things to say! But again, nothing will be as compelling as opening your own eyes and seeing who he is. The answers are always there.

Here it is in a nutshell, so tiny that you can put it on a bracelet (or not, everyone has their own taste). The crucial and undeniable point is:

WHAT YOU GOT IS WHAT YOU'LL GET

This is worth repeating. *What you got is what you'll get.* He has already shown you who he is. If he plays video games all day and hates nature, drop the fantasy that you will move off-grid to a tiny house in the woods to compost and procreate via moonlight. Why? Because…what you got is what you'll get.

Once we have clearly identified who someone is, the real work begins by sitting on your hands and biting your tongue. It is not your job to change someone, and it doesn't work anyway. Not in the long run. You can't transform someone into "your" perfect guy, and trying to do so is time-consuming, mentally exhausting, and selfish. By attempting to change someone, you're telling him he is not good enough as he is. You are informing him that your way is the right way, and he is wrong. You want him to change to make *you* feel better!

Let us say that again:

By attempting to change someone, you're informing him that your way is the *right* way, and he is *wrong*! You want him to change to make *you* feel better!

Did that hit you in the gut like it did us? We know you wouldn't want someone *not* to be who he is. You like him, and you want it to work out. If only he would plan a little bit better. Or be more romantic. Or call more. Or fill in the blank.

Instead of trying to do something to change what is, we suggest that you do nothing. Welcome it all. Open your eyes and look for the patterns because **what you see is what you get.** If a guy tells you that he doesn't believe in marriage, don't delude yourself into thinking, "Yes, but that was before he met me." There may be one man in a thousand who changes his mind, but do you really want to play Russian Roulette with your time in hopes that he's that one? Whose fault will it be in five years when he still won't marry you? Will you act shocked and be resentful when he reminds you what he has made clear the entire time?

Truth: We have done it too. However, almost ALL the women we speak with bemoan what "he did to me." Much to their dismay, in nearly every single case there was a clear sign in the beginning. Or he told them straight up who he was and what he wanted. The women choose not to listen.

There is freedom in realizing that you won't ever need to change any man to get what you want because *your* person will match your needs. If you have grown to want different things over the course of an existing relationship, that may no longer be true. But this chasm never appears out of the blue. There are clues months and months before the end to indicate that the two of you are playing ball on separate fields.

If you cannot tolerate smokers, don't date a smoker. And if you do date a smoker, don't go on a mission to get him to quit.

"Oh no, he's smoking again. I'm going to buy him some patches today and demand that he wears them, or I won't have sex with him until he does." Sounds crazy, doesn't it? But if you're honest with yourself, you may find a version of this in you.

If you want kids, and your gorgeous first date finds kids incredibly irritating and has no plans to put his swimmers to use, we strongly caution you: Don't go on a second date! That second date will lead to a fifteenth, by which point you'll find yourself sucked into a long-term relationship that you won't be able to leave because you "love him."

If you choose to throw caution to the wind, say "screw it" because he's too cute, and go for it anyway, don't blame him when he tells you (again) that he doesn't want to have kids!

Yes, people do change. However, real and lasting transformation requires an enormous amount of work, as those of us who have done extensive self-examination will attest. It's a long-term commitment that occurs when someone *wants* to change—and not because someone else wants him to. It comes from within and not because it is requested, demanded, or required.

It's hard enough to end relationships. We're human, and we get attached to people. We start to care about them. They're so good-looking, the sex is fantastic, they make you laugh constantly, and you don't believe you can be without them. There are a million reasons not to leave when we love someone. But sometimes, we must walk away before it's too late. Therefore, it's imperative to look at what you are getting into from the beginning.

We are certainly not here to tell you who is or isn't right for you. Now and again, the worst guys we've ever dated served a distinct purpose and provided invaluable lessons. But we also relinquished many who smelled of trouble from the first encounter. We walked away. We saved our own time, the most precious thing we have in the world.

We are on your side and want you to get everything you want. We want you to be loved, adored, romanced, and treated like a queen. That is why it's vital to let him be so that he can show you who is really is without interruption.

By interruption, we mean…

- Calling if you haven't heard from him
- Sending him a text (yep, calling and texting are the same)
- Making the dinner reservation because you're afraid he'll forget
- Inviting him for Christmas, Thanksgiving, *and* your birthday
- Dropping by the Starbucks you know he goes to every morning
- Coercing him to commit to being exclusive

Those are merely a sliver of the activities we engage in to put ourselves at ease. We receive a sense of security, but we won't see what he *isn't* doing. So, why should you not interrupt him in any way, shape, or form, even if it's really uncomfortable? Because if you do, you will never know what he would have done of his own free will.

We interrupt because the waiting and the information-gathering can be painful. Of course, we don't want to sit in that place. But to see who he truly is, to gather that intel, we must observe what he *does*.

CHAPTER SEVENTEEN

PLAY NO GAMES

Have you ever accidentally stumbled upon a "how to manifest your guy to chase you" Jedi mind trick? We say "stumbled upon" because it happened after you didn't purposefully *try* to do anything. For example, you decided you were done with a guy. You were out. Walking away. You hadn't told him yet, and suddenly, out of nowhere, he started incessantly calling, texting, and/or otherwise chasing you. He'd never done that before, and your mind was blown. You were confused and thought, "Oh my gosh, he really does like me!" The conviction with which you declared "I'm out" immediately left, and you resumed life as it was.

From that point on you tried repeatedly to recreate whatever you did that resulted in this attentive behavior. After all, it worked before, so it could work again, right? Maybe you had some moderate success with it.

Or, you added something else into the formula and discovered which parts worked better than others. You began feeling more hopeful that you had cracked the code.

You can play that game until the cows come home (where were they?), but unfortunately, they (the cows) always go back out to wherever it is that cows go.

Are you following? If you're as lost as those cows seem to be, let us state it in plain English: If you need a game to get him, you will need a game to keep him. Or keep him interested. Or keep him chasing you. Or keep him desiring you. Or keep him on his toes. Or get him to commit.

You cannot create your desired relationship through games or manipulation. It might feel like it's working because it can—for a brief moment in time. But the fix is temporary. Our message and the soul of this book are built on your ability to finally LET GO and stop feeling like you must become someone you are not or do anything out of the ordinary to get him (and keep him). You are ENOUGH, just as you are.

If he needs a game to stay…next!

"But isn't dating sort of like a game?" you may be asking.

Yes, there is a dance. There is a rhythm. There is a flow. We like to think of it more as a game of ping pong—the kind of harmless, fun game you played in your family room growing up. Not the kind of game you played with your sibling when you smashed the ball as hard as you could at his or her face. Ping. Pong. Ping. Pong. Back and forth. If he calls, return the call. If you call, *wait* for his return call. Do not call, call, call, and call, wonder, "Where the hell is his call back?" and then proceed to leave him six messages an hour.

We are the prize for a man. We are the queen, and he is our king (before you begin a diatribe about feminism, let us finish). To be the prize, we must have undeniable, impenetrable, full-throttle self-respect. We must know that we are worthy of love and that we are a catch.

As we have said, you can't trick energy. When self-respect emanates from you, you will attract the right guy. There is a vast difference between playing a game by trying to make a guy jealous by flirting with his co-worker and becoming and behaving as the queen you inherently are. These are two different energies: One comes from fear, and the other comes from self-confidence. And no judgement if you are coming from fear, you will just need to refocus your energy.

This type of reboot and queen-esque behavior really can draw bees to honey. In other words, prepare for him to come after you and give you more attention than you ever thought possible. Why? Because doing so makes you feel genuinely empowered. When we live our lives to our highest and most joyful potentials, the right guy will know he has found someone spectacular. Remember, you cannot fool energy or intent, and knowing the difference is one of your superpowers.

The only way we can honestly stick to our guns and not gameplay (trust us, we have tried every single other method) is by focusing on ourselves. We expect to lose you here for a moment, but yes, we will queue up the annoying self-help discussion, starting with self-love.

A PERSON CAN ONLY LOVE ANOTHER WITH THE SAME AMOUNT OF SELF-LOVE HE OR SHE POSSESSES.

How can we have respect for someone else if we don't have it for ourselves? How can we know honesty if we aren't honest with ourselves? *Be* the qualities you wish to attract. We know. We have all heard that way too often. Isn't there another way? Sadly, no. If you are a lazy sloth who doesn't take care of yourself physically, do you think an uber-successful, fit guy will find you appealing? Please answer honestly.

This is *our* role in the relationship equation: We must be everything we want in our dream man. So, get started being the best you that you can be.

"What about dating rules? We know they exist; don't lie to us!" you scream.

Of course, there are specific "guidelines" to dating, just as there are with anything else. But there aren't rules, per se. The only rule, if you must call upon one, is to be painfully aware of the differences between men and women. Understanding the nature of men is crucial, and that is why many dating experts suggest that a woman refrain from calling, give a man space, and let him come to her. They don't ultimately do so because it's a game but rather because it works *with* who they inherently are. Men like to choose the woman they want and never feel forced. They like the hunt.

The key is knowing that any man would be lucky to be with you. YOU ARE THE PRIZE. Is this anti-feminist? Some might believe so, but we continue to choose to go with the river's flow, not against it. Men hunt. They fight wars. Their need to do so is in their blood. They are conquerors. That is their nature. It's not that women can't also be these things, but remember, we aren't looking for loopholes. Men fall for women they have spotted and chosen. Women who come on to men, frequently throwing themselves at them, may get a date and even hook one of them as a boyfriend, but these men are often a little less interested, and they will continue to scan their surroundings for the "spark."

BE THE SPARK.

This doesn't mean that a woman can't proactively ask a guy out. But recognize that, in doing so, you're going against the genuine nature of men. While we are not here to tell you what you should or should not do, we've learned that it serves us to see what a guy will do of his own free will. Sometimes, he never asks you out. Isn't that something you want to know? Do you want a man who either was not willing to take a risk in asking you out or simply wasn't that interested? The reality sometimes sucks, and we sometimes hate it, but remember, we are looking to save time and see the truth.

Circling back to games, if you are your complete and true self at the beginning of the relationship, you get the luxury of continuing as yourself. You continue to be who he wants: YOU! If you managed to trap him with games, nagging questions will linger in your mind about why he is with you.

Neither unavailable men *nor* unavailable women can ever be fully present. They have a bottomless pit of need. The simple things are never satisfying, and they feed off the concept of more. More tricks. More needs. More wants. This can make even the most confident woman insecure and needy as she desperately tries to get or keep him. If you find yourself in this cycle, instead of beating yourself up, simply acknowledge where you are and then examine your *own* unavailability. If you are attracting it, you are most likely comfortable with it, consciously or unconsciously.

CHAPTER EIGHTEEN

RECOGNIZE THE HIT RATIO

When the Hit Ratio theory emerged, it was as if a new world materialized. This theory is similar to the game "I Spy" that you likely played as a kid. Someone else says, "I Spy…a Volvo." As your eyes ping open in the back seat of your parents' car on your way to your annual lake house vacation, Volvos are suddenly everywhere. Sedan Volvos, SUV Volvos, regular Volvos. Who knew they still even made Volvos?

The Hit Ratio is the same. If you open your eyes, you will find him everywhere. "What is a Hit Ratio guy?" you may be wondering. A Hit Ratio guy hits on woman after woman but doesn't care which one he ultimately lands. In other words, whichever woman he lands isn't unique. This guy simply aims to land any pretty girl for a hook-up, relationship, date, or distraction, and he casts his net to see who he can reel in.

Something may be nagging at you at this point. You may be ruminating, "But of course, men like the physical aspects of a woman." Yes, they look around; they're men. They are visual. A man usually first identifies someone because of a physical attraction, which leads to a potential spark. He then moves in for the kill. Unfortunately, the kill can end up being little more than a warm body to pass the time with at night. She's not necessarily going to translate into his soulmate or future wife. So, yes, attraction has to be there. But we want to avoid a guy for whom any girl will do. We want the guy who says, "It has to be *you*!"

The easiest Hit Ratio guy to spot is the one typically flirting at the bar or party. He will ask any girl in his personal space if she wants a drink or wanders over to her. We're talking about the smarmy, douchey, roving-eye guy in the movies. "Hey there, gorgeous" is handed out like KitKats on Halloween. But that's the caricature version, and we're pretty sure you aren't falling for him. (Though maybe one or two have slipped through the cracks. It happens to the best of us.)

Other Hit Ratio guys aren't quite as obvious, but you can spot them if you have your eyes open. He might be smart, sexy, charming, and everything else you desire, but there's another quality you can decode—if you're attentive to details. Maybe he's friendly to you and *all* your friends, even to the extent that you have no idea which one of you he likes. Or it's clear that he wants you specifically, but his interactions with your girlfriends begin to feel inappropriate. If you watch closely, you'll start to suspect that he's interested in them too.

At this point, you'll become infuriated, and your first impulse will likely be to get other women out of the way. We aren't talking about taking out a hit on them. We mean that you'll have an absolute, deep-down, unrelenting urgency to keep them away from him. We've discussed removing the problems seen in patterns before they become problems you can't easily walk away from. Unfortunately, your inner alarm should be about removing *him*, not her. We usually have it backward.

Hit Ratio guys who can be less obvious become even stealthier. Like ranks in the military, they all have different areas of expertise. Sometimes you won't even notice, at least not right away. But deep down, you know; you're trying to override your intuition. Maybe you think you and a guy have a relationship blossoming, and you're desperately trying to bury what you saw:

- The girl you caught him smiling at for a bit too long
- The four girls you knew were seemingly too chummy with him
- His constant calls to the girl in your study

group
- Hearing him saying the same things to you that you overheard him say to another girl
- The inappropriate social media interactions that even your friends have addressed

At this point, you'll probably start to feel a bit crazy. You'll begin to wonder whether he really *does* like you. Are you special? Sure, why not. But so is the other girl (or girls). Why? Because he is utilizing the Hit Ratio. If you vanished from his life, another girl would quickly fill your place. Which, again, means that you aren't special in his eyes. We don't say this to hurt you. We say it to help you. Once you know what he's doing and that you aren't his only focus, it will be easier for you to let him go.

How can you best prepare for this? How do you know if he is looking for any girl or if you are *the* girl? It requires focus and eyes wide open. You must have the patience to sit back, hear his words, and—most importantly—watch his actions.

A man is linear in his thinking. When he wants you and only you, he will pursue you (and only you). He'll go to the ends of the earth because he won't be able to stop thinking about you. Once you have gotten into his head, there will be no getting out. This is a very different scenario from a man doing his Hit Ratio dance to find his take-out and movie chick for the next few months.

We want to be unique in a man's eyes. We want to be with a man who knows and loves every little piece of us. He doesn't have to *like* everything, as we are sure we won't like everything about him. But he should adore us because of the little things, the way we laugh, if we need a certain type of spoon to eat cereal, or the number of times we need to check whether the door is locked before we go to bed. These little quirks are what make us who we are.

Standing out instead of blending in requires knowing ourselves, quirks and all, and accepting ourselves. When you completely value who you are, it will become vital for you to have a man who values you with the same intensity. You will not settle for anything less than that, and you most certainly will not settle for someone playing a numbers game.

Sara's Story

I used to hang out with a girl named Lena, who was blonde and blue-eyed, and as far as men were concerned, we were the same person. Lena, oh Lena. For years, she was the bane of my existence. Repeatedly, men guilty of utilizing the Hit Ratio had a thing for me and then for her (or vice-versa). Although the Cindy Crawford Rule was good in theory, the overlapping of these men's sensibilities was too much to stand. I started going out of my way to manipulate the situation to keep her far away from whomever I was dating at the time. If she even said hello to someone I was involved with I would give her the cold shoulder. I couldn't stop it. Even knowing what I knew, I became the woman I said I wouldn't become.

Once, she approached me and a guy I was dating at a coffee shop. She said hello, and I wanted to push her right into the cappuccino machine. I was livid that she would do that—say hello. The audacity! Of course, my fear had nothing to do with her because, in truth, I was trying to hold on to someone who wasn't mine.

Years later, after I got married, she became friends with my husband. Interestingly, these feelings were never triggered because they didn't need to be.

CHAPTER NINETEEN

KNOW YOUR
MAN-MUST-HAVES

You, of course, *can* choose to stay with a guy you know isn't great. We have no idea what you might learn from any of your relationships. Some of our greatest lessons came from our worst boyfriends and overall shitty life decisions. So yes, you *can* learn and grow from being with a less-than-stellar guy.

However, you can also gain wisdom and clarity from going to prison; it doesn't mean you *need* to go there. You don't need to spend five behind bars to deeply understand how essential and life-affirming freedom is. Still, if you do go, you certainly will get that gift! We all have used the hackneyed saying: "Hindsight is 20/20." We rattle it off when we make mistakes, miss cues, or forget something. But in the context of relationships, looking back does give us the greatest gift of all: clarity.

That guy from college you found in bed with your roommate? He gave you the gift of knowing that your number-one requirement may be loyalty. And now, armed with that number one non-negotiable, you can eliminate prospects without the loyalty gene. The guy with the roving eyes? Out. The guy who suggests a polyamorous relationship? No thanks. The guy who cheated on his ex? Nope. Sometimes there's more work to do than that, but if you are looking for loyalty, choose to date a man who:

- Doesn't keep you a secret and wants you to be entirely out in the open to his friends and family
- Wants a relationship
- Has had meaningful relationships in the past
- Is loyal and believes in monogamy

How are you going to get what you want if you don't *know* what you want? We tend to find out what we want by experiencing precisely what we don't want, and once we identify something we do NOT want, we get to choose not to go there again. If you think back to past relationships, you will discover a beautiful and glorious tapestry of all your desired and required must-haves.

Clarity is often the most significant gift you can receive in the wake of the wrong relationships. Maybe you learned that you love romance and sweet gestures from the guy who refused to hold your hand in public because of his no-PDA conviction (the same guy who thought Valentine's Day was created by Hallmark). If you spent five years with a slob who used every available space in his house to pile his dirty clothes, you probably wouldn't jump into a future relationship with a hoarder.

Although you may have repeated past blunders and needed a second (or twentieth) attempt to finally learn the lesson, you can change your circumstances and patterns in a moment. When you realize—through trial and error—that "Mr. Cheap Ass" is not your type, you will hopefully run for the hills when a guy asks you to pick up the tab on the first date because he is saving for an X-Box. A generous guy would beg the GM of the restaurant to let him wash dishes before he'd let a woman pick up the tab upon a first meeting. (And, for the record, appreciating an old-fashioned man who treats you to dinner does not make you a gold-digger or an anti-feminist.)

Bear in mind, most of us have a habit of tossing all our newly declared boundaries out the window when XYZ bad-boy appears over the horizon on his Harley. Still, if you remain diligent, you can do this.

As we previously stated, we are not the girls who will have exercises at the end of each chapter, but we're going to stray from that for one quick second and encourage you to whip out a pen (or a keyboard).

It's list time!

We did not invent the following list idea; it's been around longer than reality television. However, it clarifies what works and what doesn't by digging through our experiences and examining the life we have lived. You may, theoretically, love men who cook. Who doesn't? But if you haven't experienced a guy who does absolutely nothing in the kitchen, it may not ring the "must-have" bell.

Write down *every single one* of your must-haves. When you review them later, certain items will shine more brightly; those are your true must-haves. Don't think of it as a tedious task. Have a good time with it. You can skip this step, but this activity is incredibly fun, and that's coming from two girls who abhor any type of homework.

To get started, think about your last catastrophic dating situation. Let's say the guy was an alcoholic. If that were the case, perhaps your list will include: "My guy socially drinks." If you want a guy who has a specific profession (and it's non-negotiable), put it on the list. If you want a guy who has not yet had children (but if he has, it's not a deal-breaker), take note of it. Jot it down in a "not a deal-breaker" section.

List everything as a positive. If you have learned from your past experiences that lateness irks you, list "punctuality" as a must-have. It should be clear and detailed, and it should include your preferences in the areas of:

- Monogamy

- Romance
- Spontaneity
- Fun
- Travel
- Chemistry
- Spirituality
- Intellect
- Curiosity
- Compassion
- Success

We won't pretend that physical appearance doesn't matter. If you have must-haves in the aesthetic department, write them down. For example, Jacqueline won't date a guy under six feet tall. Maybe you want a man who drives a hunter green Tesla. Nobody else is in your head and knows what is or is not a deal-breaker, so cover it all. Write down the qualities you want in a partner and in a dream relationship, as well as the way you want to feel in that relationship. Keep in mind, many things in life come and go, such as cars, money, and work, so don't skimp on the qualities that don't, such as character. What type of character is essential to you?

When it's all listed out, you will see what you can live both with and without. Maybe several of the items on your list are preferences, not requirements. They can be more thoroughly sorted through later.

Be completely honest with yourself about what you want. If you want a few different booty calls and fun without commitment, great! If you want a serious boyfriend, fantastic! Many girls will say they want a serious boyfriend but then pretend a casual relationship is perfectly okay with them.

THE CLEARER YOU ARE ABOUT WHAT YOU WANT, THE MORE QUICKLY YOUR GUY WILL MANIFEST IN YOUR LIFE.

We never know exactly when our guy will show up, but if we become crystal clear on what's a yes and what's a no, we can save ourselves a whole lot of time.

But we aren't finished quite yet…

Before you put that list aside, highlight the items that are non-negotiable—the absolute must-haves. There are probably between three and six of them. Circle or highlight them.

Now, re-write your list and place those must-haves at the top. Color them or adorn them with stickers. We don't care what you do to emphasize them but make them perfectly clear. These are *your* man-must-haves.

Guess what happens once you have a list of man-must-haves? You will never again date a guy if he doesn't have these specifications. At least, that is how we suggest that you proceed.

DON'T DATE ANY MAN UNLESS HE MEETS THESE TOP-LEVEL CRITERIA.

We know it is easier said than done, but you will come to a crossroads while you may not believe it now. One day, there will be a *very* sexy man standing in front of you who possesses almost none of the must-have qualities on your list, and he will try to seduce you down the wrong road with his abs and charm. Oh yes, he will. And while you might choose to be interested, you also might very well not.

If you do cave, you will at some point return from a holiday and face the list again because Groundhog's Day is a real thing. After enough times returning to the list, you'll finally find it within you to say no to anyone who does not possess your man-must-haves. When that happens, you will feel like a warrior. You may also become annoyed or even sad when you look back on the guys you let slide through your pearly gates without possessing those qualities. Instead, you should be proud. Turning away from temptation is hard, and it takes what it takes. Ultimately, you WILL meet someone who fits not only your most essential man-must-haves but probably your entire list.

Jacqueline's Story

I am not just a healthy, plant-based, it's-good-for-my-blood-pressure vegan. I'm an ethics-based, I-do-it-for-the-animals vegan. I don't ever downplay it. Therefore, being vegan was paramount on my list—number two, in fact. Number one was "over six feet tall" (don't judge me. I'm quite tall).

But number two is still high on the list. It was non-negotiable. At least six feet tall, vegan (or at least willing to try it), faithful, kind, protective, and funny. Those were the "must-have six," and I never deviate from absolutes. If he cheated on his wife, he was out. If he was too serious and had no sense of humor, he was gone. (There could only be one of those in the relationship, and I had that role.)

Then I met Jordan. He was a hunter.

Jordan was from a Texas oil family, intellectual and liberal but a little too country for my New York ways. Forget my New York ways; it was my PETA ways that had the problem. I judged people who were vegan and then ate meat again, and I judged hunters.

But Jordan was *so* good, so tall, so well-spoken. There had to be some type of workaround. Non-negotiable couldn't mean *totally* non-negotiable, right? I indulged every single rationale: killing it and eating it is more respectful than just buying it already cut and chopped into cutlets at your local market. It's how he grew up. It's cultural. Maybe this would teach me compromise and tolerance. Could it be a good thing? After a solid five months of bullshit justification (and being called out by my friends), I knew that when he was going home to meet his dad and brother for a quail hunting trip, I no longer could delude myself. Though hunting works for others, it doesn't work for my beliefs. However, this relationship taught me that I didn't have to be black and white. If someone eats meat, it's their choice. Full freedom. And if I want someone to respect me, I need to offer that same type of respect and freedom to them.

So, I had to ask myself, *What am I willing to let go of to get what I want?*

Whether you carry this list around with you or tuck it away, you must know your Man-Must-Haves.

When your list is in black and white, it's nearly impossible to deny it if someone is not your "Mr. Right." Yet even when a guy has only four out of forty-seven characteristics you want, you might decide that you like him regardless (the mind is sneaky like that). When this happens, there are two things you can do:

- Check your list and be honest with yourself. Is he really "fun and loving," or are you pretending he is because you really want him to be The One? Is spirituality no longer a requirement, or are you changing your mind because he is not spiritual?

Remember, you are doing this for *yourself*, and sometimes we all need to shake ourselves back to our senses.

- Commit and decide to move on if he is not the guy described by your list. No overthinking, no debating, and no sidestepping. It will suck, but deep down, you'll know that you want *your* perfect guy, and this one is standing in the way.

You get to choose anyone you want, so why not go for what you *really* want. We must remember this when dealing with a red herring (someone or something meant to distract us). Who knew that a simple piece of paper could save us from so much trouble!

Sara's Story

I was once "privately" dating a guy I really liked. By "privately," I mean that I was a secret. He said he didn't want to commit, and in fact, I was "his friend." Despite these apparent and blaring signs, I still found myself torn up enough over him to unload my woes onto a male friend. I was complaining that he had "pulled the rug out from under me again" (by saying he didn't want a relationship). My friend said, "No, he pulled the rug out from under you *one* time, and he just keeps reminding you of it."

Ugh. I hated him for that truth.

Then he asked me what I wanted, and in return, I said that I wanted a boyfriend. He then advised, "Then only date men who want to be in a relationship!"

Simple truths can cut like a knife, but this advice is a gift that keeps giving. It has been passed on to many girls hiding in the shadows instead of being front and center.

CHAPTER TWENTY

DO NOT OVER-CALL, STALK, OR PLEAD

If you are engaging in any level of over-calling/stalking/pleading/maneuvering/begging/upper-handing/guilting/checking-up-on, it is a sign that you are afraid to lose something that you want to be yours. Meaning he may not be yours, and you know it.

When we feel happy and secure in a relationship, we don't comb through emails and phones, frantically searching for evidence. We don't hire private investigators to follow a guy on his lunch break. We certainly don't get defensive when we're asked about it. Feeling the need to do this could be the result of one of two things:

1) This is your shit and your baggage, which means he could be innocent.

OR...

2) You know something is off, and you want to either prove or disprove this theory with every fiber of your being.

If you chose door number one, you'd better commence some serious work on yourself. No guy is in your life to handle your fears and insecurities, and you could very well end up driving a great one away if you haven't already worked through these...what we like to call...quirks. No guy wants to have to reassure someone repeatedly, nor does he want to feel as though you don't trust him. He doesn't need to prove anything to you, and if you try to make him, he will undoubtedly grow tired of it.

If you tell Monty you've chosen door number two (that's from "Let's Make a Deal", for those of you who were born after 1980), *listen to that voice*! Did he give you a reason to feel this way? If so, it's time to be honest with yourself, and as much as you don't want to admit it, you probably already know your answer.

Would *your* guy be sneaking around on you? Would *your* guy be texting other girls? Would *your* guy have a clandestine life? Remember, when you open your eyes, the information is readily visible.

Perhaps you're in heartbreak right now. If you aren't receiving calls or texts from a guy you have been seeing, dating, or are otherwise interested in, we implore you: DO NOT contact him. Instead, let him be free as a butterfly.

Holding on for dear life requires way too much effort. And sadly, it only continues. Yes, yes, we know—it worked out for your cousin's best friend in Nashville, but we are preparing based on common truths, not wishful thinking, right? Why are you clutching? Don't you want *your* guy to move mountains for you? And don't forget, if you let him go and he's meant for you, he will still be there. It is the neediness, clinginess, and fear that can drive him away.

You want to see what he would do without your interference. Don't you want to know if he misses you without the Instagram DM reminding him that you exist? The discomfort (level two) or hysteria (level eight or nine) you wish to replace with "information or action" is *your* shit, and you must quell it! Those reactions are separate from what is actually happening, and you have to acknowledge that.

This may feel harsh (it is), and it is brutal to discover that a feeling is not reciprocated. However, there is no way that your desperate calls will get him to change his mind. Once a man decides that you're not someone he wants to keep seeing, the only thing that might change his decision is your absence. That trite, stale saying is accurate: Sometimes, people only realize what they had once it's gone. If you're in the position where you're left wondering what happened and where he went, do nothing.

"But I won't be able to apologize. I won't be able to tell him how I felt. But, but, but…"

Honest question: Have you not already done all of that? Did you not already explain yourself? If not, let us be clear: Saying something once is enough! You don't need to repeat yourself. You can say that you're sorry…once. You can say that you would love to have a conversation…once. You can even say "I miss you"…once.

We know how far in different directions this pendulum swings because the two of us have been complete opposites in this area. Sara would never say what she felt, and Jacqueline said it too much. We ultimately found a happy medium: Speak your truth clearly and to the point. *Once!* He heard you. If he is your guy, he will call you back. He will want to talk. He will want to be with you. We are queens. We beg for nothing and no one.

In general, stalking, convincing, begging, and pleading are not cute, sexy, or desirable. Also, it doesn't work. What *does* work is holding your head up high and recognizing that you deserve a man who fully wants to be with you.

It feels very personal when someone breaks up with you, doesn't call, or doesn't see the relationship going the way you do. People grow out of relationships, and everyone won't want to be with us forever. This is a painful truth from which no one is exempt. Just as friendships change and friends go their separate ways, so do relationships. It is okay, and when it happens, we don't have to receive it as a personal attack.

We get to choose what and whom we want in our lives, and conversely, so does everyone else. Everyone has the freedom to make that choice. And when you find the person who wants to be in your life with the same fervor you want them to be (and you will), you will have found your relationship. Deep down, you know this. The question, as always, is, *what are you afraid to see?*

Jacqueline's Story

I chose door number one. Don't get me wrong, there were plenty of men for whom I chose door number two, but this guy never gave me a reason to doubt him. Perhaps it was because so many men wounded me before—people I trusted implicitly—only to find out they had a separate life. I needed Jake's constant and continual demonstrations of love to feel loved. Yet the more I needed it, the less he offered it. My energy repelled his desire to comfort and love me.

One day, as I was passive-aggressively pouting on the couch, he turned and made the most profound and accurate statement I'd ever heard about myself: "It's like you have a black hole of neediness." This statement stung. A lot. Not because I was insulted, but because I knew he was right.

This was my wake-up call. I'd heard it before in different ways, but this was the one that got through.

This black hole of neediness was mine to work on. As much as I didn't want to look at that wounded, scarred, vulnerable part of me, I knew that, until I did, I could never fully be in any relationship—because I would look to "him" for my well-being and security. No guy could ever give me that; only I could. And to select men who would consistently choose and re-spect me, *I* would have to choose me. Yes, I know that's a cheesy line. I fought it forever until Jake said what he said. It was a hard slap in the face given in the gentlest and kindest of ways. But it was a needed slap, nonetheless.

CHAPTER TWENTY-ONE

SIT BACK AND ATTRACT

We have had private discussions about the whole God/energy/Law of Attraction/manifesting realm thousands of times, vacillating over which path best accessed the holy grail. We've each been super manifesters and mini buddhas, chanting, *Om*ing, and vibrating all over the place, communing with nature, until we could no longer feel the cold. We were flying high and knew all the answers to life—until it all came crashing down on our heads.

That sudden breakdown was generally triggered by something the size of a gnat, a gnat that came in the form of "him" doing something wrong or not texting us promptly. Our commitment to this way of life was precarious. Sometimes we would lose our footing over a small jab by a friend or an Instagram comment that didn't seem entirely complimentary. So, the energy force (God, Goddess, or whatever else you want to call it) was apparently *not* foolproof. At least, not for us.

On the other hand, sometimes huge things broke our trust: death, depression, or an overall feeling of abandonment. That is why we are grateful we didn't release this book when we originally wrote it. We were spiritual snobs at the time. It was first written right when *The Secret* made its way onto everyone's nightstand, and we were spectacularly irritating versions of those annoying cheerleaders touting its efficacy. Every negative thought was covered by a fake hyena laugh that could scare children. It was cringeworthy. We are so grateful we fell hard from those self-constructed pedestals.

Here is an actual excerpt from this chapter in the previous manuscript (the one that wasn't released):

We create our reality with our FEELINGS. The most important thing in this process is not what we are saying about what we want but how we are FEELING about it. We must vibrate on the level by FEELING a certain way. If we have a bad experience with a particular man, and every time we think of him, we put that vibe into the universe, we will get more of this "vibe." It is similar to a boomerang—if we think bad and destructive thoughts, those circumstances are drawn to us.

Conversely, if we are optimistic and think good thoughts, those circumstances will come into our experience. This is a simple law without any judgment. What we put out, we get back.

But how does this apply to my love life and this book?

Well, if you believe that all men are cheaters and jerks, and you feel that way down to your core, GUESS WHAT? You will find more cheaters and more jerks! If you passionately hate something and have a vehement reaction to certain things men do, you will probably keep running into that situation.

It was all true. And also, shut the fuck up.

Yes, the Law of Attraction is a very real thing. We still stand by that. But who cares when you are hysterical because he went on vacation with his young, pretty assistant from work? Hearing about the Law of Attraction when the guy you've been dating for four months disappears completely (only to show up on a dating app two weeks later) will make you want to punch us in our faces. Who gives a shit about universal energy when every abandonment issue is triggered to the core, and you are in the fetal position on your best friend's couch? Skipping over your issues, fears, and feelings (spiritual by-passing) into a fake land of "Everything's fine" will have you doing little more than sobbing in bed months, years, or even decades later.

Therefore, we are glad we fell off those pedestals. We are allowed to feel and cry and get mad and over-eat Annie's vegan mac 'n cheese. If we continuously try to "do the right thing" and act stoic and unaffect-ed, we are not past it. We repeat: We are *not* past it. It will patiently wait until we feel it.

Once we feel it—the good, bad, and the ug-ly—ALL of it, eventually, it will move through us, sometimes in a quick fashion and sometimes not. Ei-ther way, in the direction we want it to go: OUT! Consider it a spiritual enema. In Buddhism, you chant twice a day and focus on your highest self. Many Buddhists are some of the happiest, most present peo-ple around. When they begin chanting, however, it is known that the "muddy hose" phenomenon will commence. This means that your life is like the hose, and it takes a minute (or much longer) to clear out the mud. In the meantime, feelings will be stirred up con-siderably. Mucky, icky water (read: emotions) will flow until pristine water streams through.

Letting the mud flow is an indispensable part of the process. Once we do that, we can feel grateful or accepting or whatever we want to feel.

Now, how the F does this energy "stuff" apply to men and relationships? Um, doesn't it apply to EVE-RYTHING about them? Energy is especially real in relationships, every relationship, with men and be-yond. Everything is energy. We are all differently vibrating energies in the world. Cars, desks, and houses have energy, yet those inanimate objects just vibrate at a much slower pace and different frequencies than humans.

We have heard all the advice:

- Attract good men into your life by appreciating their good qualities. Doing so is crucial to feel appreciation and gratitude for their exceptional qualities.

- Appreciation and gratitude are the most powerful magnets in the universe. Feeling them will draw in more of that for which you are grateful. See something you like, and say, "YES, I WANT MORE OF THAT! THANK YOU!" If you see a quality in a person or a situation you like, appreciate it, and focus on it.

- Don't dwell on negativity for too long. Notice the bad only long enough to gain clarity about what it is you *want*. Flip from focusing on bad to good as quickly as you can. Then, when you notice these qualities in others, appreciate them.

- Stop focusing and talking endlessly about the wrongs men have committed and why they suck. Stop reliving your dire dating woes and explaining to everyone who will listen why so-and-so is a selfish bastard.

- And our favorite, the shaming, which is often delivered as follows: Stop complaining. We all have lousy dating tales. We all have been through hell and back with break-ups and heartache. Find the good. You can just as quickly focus on the good things about the guy who cheated on you, dumped you, used you, or hit on your friend because, after all, he helped you get clear about what you DON'T want.

We're not sure about you, but we don't believe that simply ceasing to complain or otherwise being negative happens on a whim. Whether or not you believe that like attracts like, meekly uttering, "I won't feel this way anymore" doesn't work. And besides, if that is what you think you *should* feel, you will simply suffer. So, we are turning it around and then dropping it on its head.

Here's what we say now (again, for the record, *while still believing in it*): Feel whatever way you want. Complain if you want (for a limited amount of time). Talk about it all for as long as you want. Girls need to talk it out to make sense of it. Then, when it is out, and you have crystal-clear clarity, refocus your energy.

Perhaps that refocusing will involve looking at and appreciating the parts of him you like (amplify that). Maybe it will be time to put away your war stories so you can create a new story (more love, less hate). Or perhaps focus less time on what he isn't doing and more on you (the sure thing).

Or not.

You are exactly where you are, and that place is perfect for this moment. When we refer to our own falls and say that we are grateful for them, we mean that they were the best results that could have happened to either of us because energy is constant and continually changing. Some days will be up, and some will be down. Either way, feel into it.

OUR ENERGY IS OUR RESPONSIBILITY! Said another way…YOUR ENERGY IS YOUR RESPONSIBILITY!

"That doesn't seem authentic," you may be thinking. "I want someone who accepts me for all of me. I need to be honest about my feelings. Anything else is game playing. He should be able to know how I feel." Blah, blah, blah…

The purpose of him knowing how you feel isn't to soothe you because you are not soothing and filling yourself. Your empty void is not his responsibility to fill. You can absolutely ignore this and update him on everything going on in your mind. He may listen and respond, and he may even like it (we love unicorns). But still, it is not his responsibility to make you feel soothed, validated, and filled up. That responsibility is on you.

We want to address another piece of the energy equation: the dance exchange between two people. It's important to note that we can feel when someone is trying to "will" us somehow. If you have plunged down a rabbit hole of hurt feelings, why not try a different approach? Instead of texting or calling him, try this on for size: Acknowledge that you're feeling really upset. Target that feeling. Ask yourself if there is any way you can get *back to you* right now.

How do you go back to focusing on yourself when you want something to transpire in a certain way? The answer will be different for every person, but with some digging, you can find some answers. Generally, the road will lead you around some curves and back up and over some hills until it leads to that place…you!

Sorry if that was enraging, but we had to say it. The triggers of abandonment, dismissal, being overlooked, or being ignored can lead you right to yourself if you are willing to sit through them and learn how to fill *yourself* up. Perhaps seek some therapy? Do some trauma work? Schedule a healing session or a walk in the woods? The options are there; you get to choose what feels right for you. Once you have found a way to self-heal, your energy will return to its rightful owner—*you*—which is exactly where it should stay.

Perhaps you're casually dating someone. It's not heavy emotionally, but you're wondering, "Where is he right now? Why isn't he texting?" If you find yourself in that predicament, here's a visual that may help you: Imagine you are holding an energetic ball. It's glowing and beautiful—alive and prickling with energy. He will call/text/reach out, and when he does, he's throwing you the ball. You will then respond as you feel you should. As you do, you throw him the ball.

The energetic ball is then back in his hands. If you have no ball in your hands, it is quite literally *out of your hands*. Instead of looking around for the ball to see if he dropped it somewhere, if it went straight to voicemail, or if it somehow didn't prompt a text notification (for the first time ever), spend your time focusing on you until you see that globe of magic riding through the air to you. The ball goes back and forth, back and forth. (We're aware of the balls and the irony.)

Yes, it can be challenging, but this is our work to do! We must learn to fulfill our needs so that we have something of value to give. What we are looking for in a relationship is flow. If you could tattoo one word in your mind when it comes to relationships, we'd suggest "FLOW."

When you flow with life, everything happens in a relaxed manner. There is no stranglehold on anything, no death grip, no cornering or taking hostages. No alarm is going off within us, triggering immediate action to fix a situation. There is only ease.

Understanding energy is finding freedom. But like all found freedom, there was a war that needed to be fought. You, my friend, hold the key that gets you out of the war and into the flow.

Jacqueline's Story

It was the perfect plan. My new boyfriend was coming to meet my family on our annual summer vacation together. Josh would arrive on Thursday and stay through the weekend. He was supposed to arrive at 2pm, and I planned accordingly. Well, something (a text) did show up at 2pm: "Hey, going to get in a quick hike, shower, and hit the road. See you soon!" I had been prepping all day, cleaning, making my mother insane by rehearsing what she could (and couldn't) say in front of him. I was livid. And obsessed. And confused.

Why didn't he want to leave sooner? Why didn't he want to get up at the crack of dawn and hop in his Ford pick-up and haul ass to hang out with my mom and me? I kept thinking on what "it" (the arrival time that was not up to my expectations) meant. My poor mother might as well not have been there because my head was somewhere else. With him. On his shared Waze ride. Watching him stop for gas. Then food. And then perhaps the bathroom? I was taking it personally, and in my mind, the relationship was over. He would arrive, and I would end it.

However, I knew that him not rushing to me didn't mean he didn't care, and his enjoyment of the scenic route and snacking did not mean he was dating other women. What I was experiencing was my issue, my fear of abandonment. It was hard to say nothing, but I shut up, and we had a fantastic weekend.

I think about how many times I didn't zip it up in the past. It's still something I have to fight to remember: Let him be. If I don't, all I'm doing is missing the moments of *my* life. I spent every second up until his arrival being angry about why he wasn't there sooner. At least it was only a day. In the past, I had spent years clinging to self-righteous beliefs about how he didn't do what I believed he should have.

CHAPTER TWENTY-TWO

SEX SECURES NOTHING

S ex sells.

Did that grab your attention? Good. But don't worry, we aren't telling you to sell sex. We are saying that sex is a high-voltage word that can be sold and used. In the right hands, it creates life. In the wrong hands, it creates destruction.

Pardon our small rant.

Here's what we most want to relay: You could disclose to us that you slept with five guys earlier today, and we would barely look up from our chai lattes. The only concern we'd have in this scenario would be whether that was what you *actually* wanted.

If you simply want to hook up and have fun, more power to you! However, many women don't. They might *think* they want to be a free-spirited, free-loving kind of girl. They might even convince themselves of it after not too long. But upon further analysis, they'll realize they indeed are not. They'll wonder why they became the American version of *Fleabag*. A more realistic assessment is that they were trying either to shortcut or lockdown a situation with "him."

Let's assume you do not want to "just hook up," or perhaps, you're not sure that you're comfortable with hippy-free love. Keep the following principle in mind while making your decision: SEX SECURES NOTH-ING.

Can it turn into something, allowing it to be one of those good ol' loopholes from time to time? Yes. You know, based on Jane, who screwed Jim on their first date and is now happily living with him in Santa Clarita as they await the arrival of their fourth baby. It can happen, like a dog can sometimes shit in a litter box. But as a rule, sex does not, in and of itself, make a man yours. You can emotionally extort him by *informing* him that you are in a relationship because you had sex, but you will not change what it already was.

Just getting a man into your bed is not a win. For the most part—and yes, this will sting—getting a man into bed is not that difficult. Did he choose you that night? Yes, he found you desirable. Maybe you have that kind of off-the-chart, slam-you-up-in-the-bar's-bathroom-wall level chemistry—that lust and "connection" movie sex scenes depict. It still procures nothing. This isn't a bank loan. You don't get guaranteed interest for opening your legs.

We know you just want him to commit to you already. You want him to be more than a booty call. If you want him to be your boyfriend, recognize that sex will not get you there. It *could*, yes, but we are not talking in loophole terms. We will assume that loopholes are in a box with winning lottery tickets for this chapter's sake. Sex is separate from commitment.

Don't worry if you have already had sex with the guy you hope to be in a committed relationship with! You didn't do anything "wrong," and remember, you can't lose what's yours. Regardless of your current situation, we are going to take sex out of it. For now, we're only asking you to ignore the two-souls-in-one connection that you two share in bed. Let's get *out* of bed for this conversation.

We have some questions…

- Did you get the commitment you wanted *before* you went all the way?
- Does he see only you (if this is a requirement, of course) or others too?
- Is he open about your relationship in his life? Do his friends know?
- Is he open about you on social media, or is he commenting with kissy face emojis to every girl who posts on his wall?
- Does he WANT a relationship?

Hopefully yes, but perhaps…no? Let's assume you didn't have these conversations before you laid down next to him. It is never too late to have them. But moving forward, it will be easier for you to have this chat with him first. Doing so will probably save you some painful moments.

Does anyone really know what the "right" thing to do is when it comes to sex? No, and quite frankly, everyone is different. Innumerable books have been written about how to snag a man. The focal point of many of them is when do you give up the coveted treasure (AKA, have the sex)?

A popular suggestion is to wait for three months before things get sexual. Others protest that once you hit your thirties, that's an outrageous amount of time, and three dates will reveal whether you want to get naked. Personally, we tend to split the difference and say that a month is an appropriate time to wait (and yes, we too thought that was insane and tried to disprove the theory).

At that time, a middle-aged therapist we viewed as a complete prude who arrived on the Mayflower was steadfast about a waiting period. She argued that there was a strong possibility you wouldn't even like who you were dating after thirty days. That in most cases, he'd fall away without your having slept with him, at which point you'd be thrilled you didn't.

And—hold onto your yoga bra—she was dead-on correct!

Use this month to listen to your inner voice. *Really* listen, watch for signs, and don't get caught up in the sheer fantasy of this man. Sometimes we don't look because we don't want to know. Or we see the truth and come up with a full Emmy-award-worthy limited series about how he is not really the way he appears to the naked eye. Regardless of your attempts to self-delude, if you look for who he truly is and believe what you see, you'll weed out many prospects.

No one can tell you what is "right" or "wrong." Listen to *your* feelings. If you feel that he is acting like a good boy just to "conquer" you, listen to that voice. Many men can put on an excellent front to get what they want. In fact, we would challenge you to not even tell him he is on a thirty-day restriction. That knowledge is for you! For the record, you may extend out to two, three, or six months if you want. The crucial reason for us suggesting a month is to see what this "thing" is between the two of you.

"I can ask him, right?" you wonder. Yes, you can. But again, people can be or say anything for a certain amount of time (and that time can include years). You can only discern the truth by tapping into your intuition and carefully watching a guy's actions. That is why it's imperative to evaluate how you *feel* the relationship is progressing. If he only appears interested in trying to get you into bed...bye-bye.

If you want a commitment from a man, it's best to obtain that commitment before sex. Don't attempt to have sex to get him to be monogamous or assume that because he is sleeping with you, he isn't sleeping with anyone else. If that's something you want, you need to vocalize it. The more you respect what you want and what works for you, the more he will. If you've already had sex, separate yourself from it and start listening and watching. Does he want a relationship? You'll already know if you've been paying attention.

It is easy to use sex to get what we want: attention, validation, and love. However, that "love" isn't *really* love. There's a high we receive when someone wants us, especially someone we lust after or deem essential. There is a reason women like bad boys. When they focus on us, we feel like we have "won." But we have won nothing because sex won't make him ours.

Are you using your sexuality to "get" the desired outcome? An outcome that might not exist without it? We want our perfect desired result, and these are as varied as Starbucks drink combinations. In the case of both love and Frappuccinos, we each must figure out what it is that we *really* want.

Here are some simple guidelines to figuring out if you are okay with deciding to sleep with your guy sooner than later:

1. Have an idea of the commitment you want *before* you have sex. Don't hope things will change because you were horizontal in bed. Sex does not change who and what he is or how he treats you.

2. Try to wait for thirty days. We are not telling you to play games and hold sex over his head like a cheat day after you drop ten pounds. You don't want him to act the way he thinks you want him to act to

get what he wants. Keep those details to yourself. This is your time to get to know him and see if the relationship is something *you* want to continue.

3. Know very clearly that sex isn't love. It does not shortcut the process of getting a relationship. **Sex is an extension of love and affection, not a means to it.** If you can't talk and get to know each other before sex, what makes you think love and affection will still be there after the lust wears off?

Before we close this chapter, we need to talk about something significant, something that is often overlooked: Is a guy worthy of *you*? We often get caught up in the excitement of being desired. Nothing feels better than seeing a guy you have been lusting after at work for the last two months finally pay attention to you. Most of us have a flood of endorphins and excitement wafts over us with that hit. But here's the thing: It's not good enough.

Is he—and we don't care who "he" is—worthy of *you*? Does he make the cut? Does he treat you properly? Adore you, cherish you, and show you off to the world?

You are a masterpiece. You are gorgeous, funny, and talented. You're a catch! If he can't see that in *and out* of the bedroom, he's not worth it. Remember, you are a queen, and not just anyone can earn the honor of entering your castle (pun intended). Shift your focus back to you, and only allow into your life those who see your magic. This could not be truer when it comes to sex because sex is *your* life-force energy. Feel your power because your power creates worlds.

Sara's Thoughts

I detest shaming, canceling, and anything bully-related. I especially dislike slut-shaming. Sex can bring up so much for a person, and it's an area that should be handled very gently. One person's sexual awakening is, to another person, a disgrace. That's why I feel this chapter should be used as an intuitive guidepost. For some, sex has been used as a weapon or to assure an outcome. To others, it may be scary and yet unrealized. So, here's what I'll say—do what you want, and most definitely trust your gut. Utilize the topic to find out where you stand in his eyes and your inner wisdom to discover how you are using it (if at all) to affect how you stand in his eyes. Are you trying to secure him? Are you using sex to hide? What has your pattern been?

I will never be the person to say you have to follow a certain rule or you aren't doing it right. I will never say you can't have sex with that stranger or that you messed up by asking him out. Do your thing, be yourself. I don't think I'm "right" and others are "wrong." You have your own issues, challenges, and lessons playing out (if you're willing to look for them).

No one gets to tell you what is right for you and your body. No one.

CHAPTER TWENTY-THREE

KNOW MR. WRONG FROM MR. WRONG

Advice is exceedingly easy to dispense to others, especially when you have a fire of belief behind the words you're preaching. The heat that accompanies your guidance comes from common sense, wisdom, life experience, or simply your run-of-the-mill opinions. People love to be right, and everyone *thinks* they're right.

We live in our own little "Truman Show" world, chockfull of rules and regulations. It works for us—which we love to let others know—because it's all *we* know. People, therefore, love to tell others what they think regarding their dating life or the relationship they're in.

"He's an asshole." "You are ruining your life." "He will never be tamed." On and on it goes.

It's one thing to dish out obvious advice. It is a

whole other ballgame to be living it out. Meaning, if you are dating a guy who's patronizing and rude to you, common sense says, "Duh, time to go," but the heart says, "Whoa, slow down. Maybe we can work this out. Is he really that bad? If I didn't A, B, or C, he probably wouldn't have had that big of a reaction. Maybe work is super stressful this week, too?" We look for anything to justify the outcome we want.

Matters of the heart are complicated. While we will *never* endorse staying in an abusive relationship, there's a reason people stay when they should run for the hills. When we want what we want (him), we can easily overlook some things. It's as simple as that. Thankfully, we have our loyal friends, therapists, and family who chime in (asked or not) with their "perspective." But ultimately, unless we get dumped or ghosted, we must decide for ourselves and by ourselves.

Choosing to leave a situation you don't want to leave is excruciating. But suppose you separate the reasons for leaving into objective categories and attempt to detach from your heartstrings, you know, the ones that are constrictor-knot tied to his. In that case, you can see the truth a bit more clearly. Just as we believe there is a Mr. Right for you, there are potential Mr. Wrongs. Here are the two very different types of Mr. Wrongs:

1) Mr. Wrong: He isn't right for you but is suitable for someone else.

OR...

2) MR. WRONG: He may be abusive—verbally, physically, or emotionally. He is perhaps an active drug addict, alcoholic, cheater, and of course, we can't leave out...married.

The Mr. Wrong who isn't right for you (but perfect for someone else) falls into the category not necessarily of "Mr. Across-the-Board Wrong" but of "Not Your Guy." Most men fall into this category: the hot guy you blew off after your third date, your high school boyfriend who married his college girlfriend, that first serious relationship you were sure was your forever one, or that guy from the gym who is your perfect astrological match. There are billions of men on the planet (literally). Not everyone is going to be the piece that fits into your unique puzzle.

As Sigmund Freud said, "Sometimes a cigar is just a cigar." Everything doesn't have to have a hidden meaning. Just because a man doesn't pay attention to you doesn't mean he's gay. He's not mean or an asshole if he doesn't want to date you or finds your friend more attractive. He is simply not right *for you*.

If a guy wants to live a life of leisure without stress and commitments, it doesn't mean he is a man-whore or a player. He may want a woman who is more go-with-the-flow and okay with his non-committal ways. That woman might not be you, and that is okay. We don't have to make him bad or wrong. He will be who he is, and that is, quite simply, not your guy. This is, in fact, fantastic news because you won't squander time on guys who aren't for you. Your work is to trust this and let him go so you can find *your* ideal guy.

Now, let's talk about Mr. Across-the-Board Wrong. If he is abusive—verbally, physically, or emotionally—he is not your guy. There is no secret to the concept that "if he does it once, he will do it again." Even if he begs and pleads and promises, it is still more than likely that whatever happened will happen again because that is his pattern, and it is who he is. Deep down, you know this.

While we will not condone any type of abuse, we know that a sticky situation can be complicated and nuanced. Abusive men can be some of the most charming fuckers you'll ever meet. They have a bad side but can swing to sweetness, romance, and affection faster than they can pack a punch. If you find yourself in this situation, get out or get help (if you can't get out). We know that nothing is black and white, and we know that you care about him—feel bad for him even—but it won't get better. Abuse only gets worse.

No one has the right to cause you injury or harm. No fist or threat should ever have a part in your relationship. We all fight, and those fights can get hairy at times. But does it go too far? It's essential to learn how someone fights. Does he have a nasty streak? Does he scare you? People have arguments, get angry, and even yell. But there is a difference between clearing the air and abuse. You should feel adored, protected, cherished, and above all…safe! You should never feel like you're walking on eggshells, looking over your shoulder, or being afraid to say something wrong or that might get you in "trouble."

Jacqueline's Story

I have had my fair share of Mr. Wrongs. Generally, they fell into the highly manipulative, emotionally stunted, less-evolved and angry category: guys who were in no position to be a partner. But not all situations are black-and-white obvious. One man I was dating screamed at me for accidentally nicking his face while helping him shave off his good luck World Series beard. His apology: "It's not like I hit you." As if this were the bar.

I never acknowledged "Mr. Wrong for Me" because I was committed to having a partner. Do I want to watch football, go to the casino every weekend, eat shitty food for dinner, go to Coachella, discuss the most remarkable modern artists, or play X-Box? No, I do not. That may be someone else's perfect scenario, but it isn't mine. Mine is more along the lines of discussing the *NY Times* editorial on Sunday, watching Bill Maher, and spending time every so often at an animal sanctuary.

I could fake it, keep that illusion of interest for a little while, even distract myself from the incompatibility. Still, I could not pull it off long-term. None of them was my guy, and it became too exhausting to keep "Mr. Wrong for Me" reeled in. Perhaps it's the kind of wisdom that comes with age, but I refuse to have one more fake conversation about the college football draft. Life is too short.

We can choose not to waste life's precious moments on someone who doesn't appreciate us and our feelings; we are deserving of respect. Respect is given and not forced—right along with all of the other things we can't "get" from someone merely because we want it. The days, weeks, and years you spend trying will rob you of your deserved healthy and happy life.

Active drug addicts and alcoholics also fall into the Mr. Wrong category. We aren't talking about sober alcoholics and addicts. We are talking about the guy who still *needs* a substance to get by, whether it's weed, alcohol, or any other variety of drugs. You can't make someone get sober; it must be a choice that they make for themselves. Have there been exceptions? Of course. Many spouses have entered rehab to save their marriage or family. However, ultimately, if he wants to stay sober, he must choose it for himself. If not, his sobriety will likely be short-lived.

Loving an alcoholic or drug addict creates heartbreak like none other. People spend decades trying to save their loved ones because there is an element of extreme danger that could very possibly result in death. This can create anxiety and trauma, which may require professional help (yes, we speak from experience). It's a painful road, which is why several books have been written on this subject alone. If he isn't ready to slay his dragons, what makes you think he will fight dragons for you? It takes a lot of commitment and drive to work on oneself. And even when you do, it can take decades to change. If you see this sign and can get out, run!

We will now pivot to the cheater. Like an abuser and an addict, when a cheater promises he'll never do it again, you'll always wonder if it's the truth. It can turn an ordinarily trusting woman into a Sherlock-Holmes-level sleuth, checking his texts and emails while he's in the shower and turning on his location finder so you can track him. If you find something suspicious and approach him about it, denial will be the usual response (well, denial and subsequent anger for not trusting him). Before long, you will begin to second-guess your sanity. With each bit of information you expose and stay in spite of, your self-esteem will be chipped away, making it harder and harder to ever leave.

Cheating is possible to work through. Anything can be worked through if both parties are willing. But it will linger. If fidelity is an essential quality on your man-must-have list, being with a cheater will be hard to get over, even if he swears it only happened one time. Believe who someone is when he shows you. If your man can be taken once, it can definitely happen again.

We know, your cousin's co-worker and her husband got through infidelity, so clearly, it's possible. Maybe after extensive therapy and soul searching, he will change because *he* wants to change, but is this something you want to have between you? Holding on to hope that he will become a faithful guy can only hurt you. Instead, make decisions that best serve *you*. Then, if he is supposed to be with you, he will grow and shift right alongside you. Of course, some women are okay being in an open relationship, and if that is the case, this man may be your Mr. Right. But if loyalty is a must-have, he is not winning any prizes.

Lastly, we will talk about the married guy. This topic is known to be a no-win situation. It's been said that men never leave their wives. This is usually true. However—and this may be controversial to suggest—sometimes they do. Some people are with the wrong people, and they don't know this until they meet someone else who stops them in their tracks. We say that reluctantly, however, so as not to offer you hope that someday he will leave her, and you will end up living happily ever after. Just as there isn't an absolute rule about when to sleep with a man, there are men who leave their wives for other women with whom they spend the rest of their lives happy (and to whom they are perpetually loyal).

A man leaving his wife for another woman in this, dare we say respectful way, is rare. He's not a full unicorn, but he's like spotting a unicorn costume on Christmas Eve. He's uncommon, but Christmas is close enough to Halloween to cause you to believe you haven't gone entirely off the rails in terms of what you think you've seen.

However, and this part is crucial, there is a right and wrong way for a man to handle this situation. A man with integrity who finds himself in this situation will find a way to deal with it honorably. He will leave his wife and *then* pursue you because of his character and the love and respect for his wife.

On the other (and more common) hand, there is the man who is faced with the dilemma of falling for someone other than his wife. He falls prey to his emotions, has an affair, blows up his family, and drags you along for the ride. Unfortunately, most adulterers want the best of all worlds. An affair is a surefire way to ensure a relationship's demise, removing the married person's sense of full responsibility. It is easier to be dramatically forced to leave than to own your feelings and make a conscious choice.

However, when a man can't choose for himself, he's also able to evade accountability. He then can avoid processing the emotions and disappointment that accompany the situation. Make no mistake. If this is how it's handled, you can be confident that this is how *all* sticky situations will be handled. How somebody acts in one area shows precisely who he or she is and will be in *all* areas.

If you've somehow stumbled into a relationship that is "different" with a married man, perhaps you've convinced yourself of things that people tell themselves to justify their actions:

"If he were in a happy marriage, he wouldn't have an affair."

"They aren't meant to be together."

"He will leave her."

"She must be a terrible wife, or he wouldn't be with me."

"She doesn't get him."

Keep in mind, if you do end up with him, you won't ever erase the thought, "If he cheated *with* you, he will cheat *on* you" from circling through your brain. The bottom line: If a man or woman knows his or her marriage is over and has been for some time, they will let their partner know. They will do the right thing. Why? Because they have integrity, and though they may not be in "love" anymore, they love their partner. They will be kind and respectful *first*.

We know you want that guy, and you don't want to know that he's the wrong one. We find a man, think he's The One, and all reason goes out the window, avoiding what we already know is a temporary fix. This denial only wastes precious moments of life.

But what if you *don't know*? You've nodded your head in agreement as you've read the list of "wrong" men. You know your guy isn't abusive or a cheater, and while he drinks, it's not enough to put him in the Betty Ford Center. This isn't registering for you. You genuinely don't want to waste your time, but you also can't see the situation clearly.

We call this "The Red Flags are on the Table."

Sara's Story

A friend named Shannon was married to a man for years. When she met him, she saw all the red flags and went against her instincts anyway, thinking she would be different. Even though she knew that he had cheated on every girlfriend he ever had, she believed him when he said he wasn't like that anymore.

Years into their marriage, she discovered that he was having an affair with a co-worker. She may not have been able to trust his word, but she remained true to her own. She'd told him that she would leave him if he ever cheated on her.

The next day when the movers came to get her stuff, he couldn't believe she was leaving. He was baffled that she meant what she said. She knew at that moment that he would never change. As hard as she struggled to make it on her own after that, she did it because she knew it had to happen. Even if she wanted to stay, she knew he would always be a cheater.

It's all there, right in front of you, laid out like a winning hand of cards. You just don't know if the other player is all in, bluffing, or ready to fold. There are "things" that don't perfectly fit your man-must-haves manifesto. He has made you cry and made you question parts of yourself. You can find justifications for how he behaved, which was terrible, but not enough to make him a clear no.

So here you sit. You're not sure what you should do, but one thing is clear: You still want him.

To make your dilemma even worse, *he* wants to be there. He wants to work on it; he wants to try. Good guys can behave poorly, but when they do, they correct themselves. So, how do you know for sure if he is the wrong guy? He's the wrong guy if he is not willing to correct himself *and* ready to change. To this, we say, "Only you will know the right move to make." If you are genuinely honest with yourself, and you're not in denial, perhaps you need more clarity on if he is willing to do the work. If that's the case, sit back and see what happens. A man who wants to try is a man who wants to be there. He is choosing you.

But...

Acknowledge, admit, and accept that you are proceeding with red flags on the table. Own that you are choosing a man who's holding red flags *despite* what you said or thought you wanted. You are deciding to move forward anyway, and if you lose time (whether a month or a decade), you'll know it was a result of *your* decision, not his.

Owning your choices in this way will free you. If you want to stay with a cheater, accept that he will most certainly cheat again, and when he does, don't feel like you were robbed of your time. This is power, the power of choice and power to change your mind. Making these decisions isn't easy, but you will always know the truth if you look for it deep inside.

Sara's Story

I remember this guy who was exactly what I wanted as far as "type" goes. I was ecstatic when he asked me out. A close male friend of mine was his friend, so of course, I immediately called said friend for his opinion. He said, "Sara, under *no* circumstances should you ever go out with this guy!" He also pointed out that he had not said that about anyone and wouldn't unless he absolutely meant it.

Even though this guy was his good friend, he'd personally known three different women he'd dated and they all said that he was a complete asshole. I thanked him for his opinion but decided I needed to get a follow-up opinion from another male friend of mine in our circle, to whom I asked, "What would you do in this situation. Dean said that I should stay away from this guy. What should I do? Do you think he knows what he's talking about?"

"Um, yes! You should listen!" he responded. Of course, I didn't listen because, frankly, I thought he was hot. I went on two dates with him, during which I saw all the signs of why I shouldn't continue to go out with him:

- He incessantly talked about himself.
- He asked me to accompany him to his house to walk his dog. When I said no, he yelled at me for being disrespectful.
- He flirted with the hostess at the restaurant.
- He told me that he could not be with someone for more than one year because he loved women too much.

All of this could have been avoided if I had trusted my friends' advice, my friends who had never *not* had my back. It's incredible what you will overlook when you want something.

Often, we think that a specific "type" is perfect because he has our ideal look or style, but that does not mean that he comes with character, kindness, or integrity.

CHAPTER TWENTY-FOUR

PLACE ALL BETS ON THE NICE GUY

We wanted to title this chapter "Nice guys won't shag your best friend (and if he does, he isn't a nice)," but it felt like too much. We needed to get to the point and double down on it: Nice guys hold the winning hand.

Most girls we've known dream of that great guy. He's fully loaded—sweet, sexy, romantic, chivalrous, and nice. Yes, we said nice. Commonly, we don't hear women vocalize the quality "nice." But when you really wish your guy would think of the idea to have your mom over for s'mores or volunteer his truck for your move or ask you if you need help cleaning your desktop clutter, all that falls into the category of "nice."

While you want your guy to be thoughtful, kind, and compassionate, you also tend to want a specific guy who is *not* nice to suddenly transform. In other words, you want your bad boy to *also* be nice. Of course, if he's a bad boy, he's probably not a nice guy. If he were, you wouldn't be with him in the first place.

The challenge is that you have no clue what dating a nice guy feels like. You've been eating candy and highly processed foods for so long that you literally can't taste how amazing real fruit is. Your taste buds are (metaphorically) fucked.

"But nice guys don't exist. They are hard to find. They are all married."

We hear your battle cries! You may believe that the existence of vampires is more probable than an available, attractive, great guy—who is also nice.

"But they aren't my type. They aren't hot. There just isn't that…thing. That spark." We too screamed that objection, so we know you will not like this, but we must say it: Nice guys are where it's at. *You* just can't see them right now. But they are everywhere!

We aren't therapists, and we will therefore keep our reasoning as to why you can't see them right now experiential. We won't delve down the bottomless well of unhealthy attachment styles and family dynamics to explain why women are sometimes attracted to a particular type—dysfunctional, non-committal, emotionally stunted, for example. There are excellent resources available to help you discover and understand the impetus to walk directly into the fire, should you be interested in them.

We chased that elusive bad boy for most of our lives, believing that we'd win in the game of life if only we could capture him. After suffering through a couple of bad boys in a row, we vowed we would change our ways. All we wanted by that point was a "nice" guy—the one who shows up with flowers, asks what type of food we want, listens fully, and asks questions when we are telling stories. We were ready, willing, and committed. The problem was, we wanted all that *and* the addictive qualities of the bad boy.

We prepared to date the quintessential "nice" guy. No more unparalleled charm. No more elusive innuendos followed by a lack of commitment and inaction. We were ready to be adults. We'd never been in a relationship with this type and didn't know what it felt like. We hadn't experienced it, so we quickly threw it all away—him *and* his flowers, erased without a second thought.

We claimed that this "nice" guy felt "off" somehow; there was nothing there, no spark. It was slightly boring, lacking in that nauseating, scintillating, desperate torture you feel while waiting for his text after twenty-four hours of no contact. We started picking out little things in the "nice" guy's personality that quickly became deal breakers. If he liked us and thought we were amazing, we couldn't accept it because it felt foreign. There was no insane chemical attraction, inexplicable rush, or crazy burst of excitement. It seemed like he could be a good friend, a loyal companion, and a trusted confidant, but we didn't consider him to be in the lover category.

Having gone through that (more than once), here's the notion we want you to chew on: IF THE BAD BOYS WHO RUINED YOUR LIFE WERE THE "RIGHT ONES" FOR YOU, PERHAPS YOU NEED TO REEVALUATE YOUR CHOICES.

Let us make it more straightforward for you: Your man picker is broken.

Ding, ding, ding!

If you think the hot bad boy is "right" when he's really wrong, maybe your picker needs an overhaul. Again, we don't want to go into professional therapist territory. Still, it's been said that the more "fireworks" you feel, the more of his "issues" you're mirroring. Your neuroses matching his neuroses equals an epic shit show.

How has your man-shopping been working out for you thus far? If you are reading this book, the answer is probably "Not very well." Since you've had limited success choosing your future husband, perhaps it's time to give something else a try?

One of the most powerful tools we have available to us, which can be applied anywhere in your life, is Flip a Bitch, also known as doing the exact opposite of what you've been doing. Can't feel your way out of a problem? Can't think of a solution? Can't for the life of you figure out where to start? Flip a bitch on its head.

What does this mean when it comes to your dating life? Go where the love is. If you go out with a nice guy and your intuition says, "Nah, there's nothing here." FLIP A BITCH. Go out with him again. And again. Attempt to go out with the "nice" guy more than once or twice (after which point you usually decide there's no chemistry). Decide to go out with him four, five, even six times. You will likely start to appreciate and even become *attracted* to someone who shows you respect and kindness. He may or may not be the person you end up with, but you will get a taste of what it feels like to be adored.

Being adored is the desired result, but you presently have zero idea what that feels like. You have associated challenges, pain, and hard-to-get with good feelings. It's a shitty drug and one that's always left you chasing it. Being adored is spectacular, and once you get used to *that* feeling pumping through your veins, you will never go back.

Adoration is the exact opposite of what the bad boy offers. He leaves you wondering, for weeks at a time, what he's really thinking. Figuring out what he's thinking, what his next moves will be, and how many more minutes it will be until you get your answer becomes a full-time job with the bad boy. You are wired to think that nervous energy is chemistry. It's not! It's merely a strong feeling, similar to being addicted to drama and getting an adrenaline rush from it. Once you let go of your need for chaos and become accustomed to peace and serenity, the thought of drama alone will repulse you.

The electric shock jolting through your body when he enters the room is not love. Love feels good. Love is kind and gentle. Love is respectful and sweet. You may not yet know what that feels like, but you will once you get enough of it. If you detox your soul from your need to have drama to feel "love," you will notice that you have a different kind of "firework" feeling for nice guys—one that won't leave you in the fetal position.

The nice guy, the one who actually *is* husband material, will make it clear that he cares and wants you. He will ask you out on proper dates again and again. And no, the bad boy who left you in tears way too many times is not going to change and treat you this way. If he's not behaving nicely, and someone who behaves nicely is what you want, he is not the one for you.

You will never look back and long for those wasted days sitting by the phone wishing and praying for a scrap of affection. You might find yourself drifting into the fantasy of an epic crazy "love story" once the dust settles. Still, once you remember all those squandered days and years trying to reform an asshole, you will shudder at the thought of doing it again.

When the "nice" guy theory permeates your being and you shift in your desires, you will only respond to men who give real love. Go out with someone loving and kind *and* an overall "nice" guy who truly *is* the real badass. When you do, you will see that every experience in which you were not appreciated prepared you for the guy who would treat you right.

P.S. To clarify, there is not a man shortage.

Sara's Story

Before I met my husband, I had a string of about five of these "situations" (and by situations, I mean the kind of undefined time spent together that often gets classified as "hanging"). I had to let go of them all because those guys simply weren't right. And that is a far kinder description. I had to walk away because I made the decision that I would not settle. One after another, I sat back and watched these guys I liked flirt with my friends, avoid commitment, check out other women, and so on. I sat back and noticed who they were. Let me be clear: it sucked! It was as if nothing flowed, and nothing would go right.

Then I met my husband. And all of the things that were missing suddenly seemed to fit together perfectly.

CHAPTER TWENTY-FIVE

LET HIM GO
(HE MAY JUST STAY)

Remember, you cannot lose what is yours. That said, we are going to call bullshit for a second to clarify that you can lose what is yours if you suck the life out of it. No one wants to be with someone who is miserable. They may for a bit, but not for long. We will assume that you are not being abusive, manipulative, always angry, or endlessly distrusting. You are not a person no one can handle.

With that said, you cannot lose what is truly yours. If you're honest with yourself, you know this. There's probably a chance the guy you are worried about—the one you got the astrological reading on to see how your moons interact—may not be The One. Are you feeling defensive? Did your gut drop with dread? Do you want to tell us why we are wrong?

Here is our hope because we promised you hope:

You may be single-mindedly so committed to keeping him (manipulating, expelling energy, worrying, keeping other girls away) that you are repelling him. It's true. A watched kettle takes a long time to boil (why the hell is that!). If you repelled him with "I need you" energy, and you then drop it by letting him go once and for all because you want the guy who's right for you, you might find that it's him after all. If you don't let go, you will never know if he is there by choice or by force.

Let us tell you a little story.

There was a fun little new-age bookstore in the East Village that we used to frequent. Among other new-age delights, they sold various candles, and for an extra fee, you could have them cast a spell on your chosen candle related to your career, love life, or health. You name it, and they would do it.

One day, a girl busted in with desperation in her voice. Her "love" candle was not working. She was angry, anxious, and could not control her manners. "He is NOT here yet, and it has been a week!" she barked to the store clerk. All of us within earshot could clearly see why she hadn't yet attracted her guy. The girl was desperate, and it wasn't cute.

She needed a boyfriend, and she was so consumed with looking everywhere for him that she probably wouldn't have noticed if he repelled from a skylight into her living room. When you're needy, you can't see clearly.

WE HAVE TO LET GO OF OUR NEEDINESS.

If you need a boyfriend, that implies that you need a man to be okay. Your life is like a cake, and you can bake any kind of cake you desire. Fudge, carrot, sponge - take your pick. A man is merely a sprinkle on the icing of your cake. He is not the cake, nor is he the flour required by the recipe. In other words, he does not make your life. He adds to it. A man is your partner and an addition to an already fulfilled and extraordinary life.

Imagine two stunning trees—one is you, one is him. Each has separate, strong roots, but their leaves have joined, making it a beautiful sight. Differently colored and shaped leaves merged, however each has its own roots imperative to its survival. We find that to be a brilliant analogy of an ideal relationship.

We've both experienced a deep need for random men who weren't worth our time. Personal growth in dating is a process and a journey. However, we aim to heal our wounds as we go because they are revealed to us in bite-size pieces, not all at once. To find a fantastic guy who can be your true partner, you want to be solid in who you are in your life first. It's akin to airplane safety instructions: You need to put on your air mask before your child's. We must love and care for ourselves before we truly have anything to give another.

No one changes overnight. We know it's not as

simple as reading a book, snapping our fingers, and instantly becoming perfect. Do you know any perfect people? Neither do we. It takes time to enact long-term change. If you are like us, you probably like fast change and want instantaneous gratification. After decades of attempting "quick fixes," we see now that what we ultimately experienced was "slow change." One tiny, sometimes unnoticeable-to-the-human-eye change after another. Change happens with each small step, not while sitting down on December 31 writing the huge transformation scenario we expect to manifest by Valentine's Day.

If you are a "caller" who likes to blow up your guy's phone ten or more times a day, declaring that you will never call again is probably an overstatement. Instead, aim to do the best you can in the area you are typically challenged—in this case, calling. If you call only two times a day, you have achieved a miracle. Call just once, and you are a next-level ninja. This is a prime example of the Flip a Bitch principle in action.

If you are heartbroken over a man and cannot conceive how to let him go, try implementing what you can. You may talk about him, cry, and remain convinced that he is The One until every friend you know patches your calls to voicemail. Who cares! If that is the best you can do not to show up at his house, kudos. Only you know what your best is at any given point in time!

Heartbreak sucks, and there is no one path to healing. We have all been in that horrible space of heart-pounding pain, crying over the man we knew was not going to be our future husband. We may have consulted our favorite healer, gotten our hair done, taken up fencing, or even engaged in Goddess Circle rituals. It doesn't matter how you do it but try to put your life back together. Do anything not to meddle in the outcome. This is the ultimate letting go of neediness. You must decide to believe that if he is your guy, he will come back.

A breakup comes with sadness and heartache, but remember that you are extraordinary, and your right man is out there making his way to you. Do the best you can to treat yourself with the most self-love possible. You can and will have an excellent relationship if you do the inner work required to get out of your own way.

CHAPTER TWENTY-SIX

SELF-WORTH: GET SOME

There is a phenomenon that presents itself every single day and remains the most baffling trend of all. It's mystifying how many amazing, gorgeous, funny, kind, and talented women simply don't see their worth. Famous actresses, scholars, CEOs, models, stay-at-home moms, company employees, and every variation in between have more in common than one might think, including:

- Insecurity
- Doubt
- Self-deprecating humor
- Guilt
- Shame

The lack of fundamental self-worth—not the fake kind that compels you to post a gazillion filtered selfies with spiritual quotes indicating how woke you are or photos of your picture-perfect family—is omnipresent. We're talking about basic self-worth. The kind that reminds you that, beyond a shadow of a doubt, you deserve and can have your heart's true desires, whether that's "him" or someone else. This awareness produces the kind of confidence that comes from knowing that it doesn't matter if your desire isn't appearing today; something better for you is on its way. Self-worth is the unshakeable "Holy crap! I am awesome" that radiates from the inside out, not the other way around. But where did it go? Did you ever have it? Did your family break it? Did a heart-break crush it? Did life destroy it? Where oh where did that shiny you go?

Some things need to be lost to be found. And if we have learned anything, it's that you can't jump from the first floor to the penthouse. This book is about baby steps. With each tiny step you take in honor of yourself, with each spoken "no" when you want so badly to say "yes," with every move in a direction that speaks to your worth, you build that worth. Before you know it, you are living in a palace fit for a queen.

If you can't go from here to there in a snap, what else can be done? We all know that most women don't get what they deserve in relationships; they get what they *believe* they deserve. This belief is not conscious. It comes from deep, deep down in the depths of our subconscious. We can't "affirmation" our way out of it either. We can't expect to be treated with respect when we don't believe that we deserve respect. It's humbling to realize that the men we choose treat us in a way that reflects the exact way we feel about ourselves.

Yes, it's a pickle. It can take years—decades, even—to heal our inner wounds. We're sure that, if you're anything like us, you've already been on this inner journey for a long time. You may even be asking, "Seriously, will I ever friggin' get there?"

Honestly, it's looking more and more like a hard "no" on that one. At least, not while we're breathing. But if you're actively working on yourself (and even if you aren't), there are some tricks you can employ that will make you feel more like the badass powerhouse you are. Whether you are pro therapy or not, we have found that after all those checks were written to shrinks and seminar organizers, the most profound results arose from one simple thing. And it's so basic and straightforward that you might overlook it: Envision the person you love most in the world in the same situation you're currently in.

Think of a female you cherish. Is it your mom, your sister, your daughter? Picture her in your mind. Would you want this person to be treated the way that your guy is treating you? Would this relationship be something you would wish for her? Someone who doesn't ask about her, makes everything about him, and is subtly abusive? Would you want someone you love to date him? Although it might not feel right to stop seeing him, doing so reflects the highest choice for your life.

You may be willing to make exceptions for yourself and run through a host of rationalizations and justifications in order to stay with him, but you would fight a dragon to its death for someone you love. You can overlook bad treatment coming your way, but if you take yourself out of it and picture your sister in your place, you will suddenly see everything quite clearly. You can separate yourself from the situation and act from logic, not emotion.

Once you do that one time, you'll be able to do it again. Before you know it, you are doing it for yourself! These are loving acts that you do for yourself. After a time of developing this habit, asking the following questions before you act becomes second nature:

- Is this action in my best interest?
- Does saying no empower me?
- Will this decision make me feel proud?

You cannot place an order for self-esteem the same way you would a new pair of shoes. It takes work, discipline, and effort. If you are willing to put in the time, build self-esteem, and consequently have unshakable self-respect, you will suddenly find yourself in a loving relationship—*with yourself!* Then that soul-quality love can manifest. Recognizing that a situation is unhealthy for you and walking away from it creates positive self-esteem because you stuck up for yourself! Add another good choice (and another, and another), and you'll be soaring with confidence. The more we don't uphold ourselves, the more we chip away pieces of our confidence. Ultimately, this lack of self-worth and self-respect can keep you in a vicious cycle of unhealthy relationships.

There is no product or "thing" you can acquire that will do this for you, yet it is the answer to the confidence you seek. If we could bottle it up and sell it as a perfume, we'd be billionaires. Unfortunately (and yet, fortunately), it can only be acquired from within.

A healthy relationship feels good. It's loving, kind, gentle, and honest. It does not include manipulation, lying, guilt, or shame. Although there are temporary fixes that may feel good in a certain moment, they do not last. When a relationship *needs* a "fix" (a call, text, or attention), it is short-lived. For instance, calling him when he isn't calling you or showing up at his favorite coffee shop may feel good until the "hit" wears off. But ultimately, you will require more, more, and more to continue feeling that way. It will never be enough.

When we have genuine, deep-down, gritty, unshakeable confidence, we don't *need* anything like a call or a text. If he's not showing up in a way that is worthy of you, you can move forward accordingly. We will never make him behave a certain way, but when we have immovable self-esteem, we will have shifted toward loving ourselves. In turn, we will be excited when the wrong person slips away.

We will no longer grasp. We will be confident. We will accept who we are. And self-love is SEXY!

Sara's Story

I once went on a double date with my guy, his friend, and his model girlfriend. To describe her as stunning would be an understatement. She had literally just shot the cover of *Cosmopolitan*. I mean, how could someone so beautiful ever have any problems, let alone lack confidence? I figured men probably threw themselves at her and proposed marriage daily. But both her beauty and my envy quickly diminished when our dates went to the bathroom, and she completely lost it.

"Where did they go? What are they doing?" she asked, as panic spread across her perfect features.

"They went to the bathroom," I replied, wondering if she somehow didn't hear them specifically say, "We're going to the bathroom." Was she asking a trick question? Her curious eyes darted quickly around the restaurant as she said things like, "I wonder what he's doing," and "I think he's calling someone." In an almost robotic state about what he was up to in the bathroom, she continued on and on. I couldn't believe it. This incredible memory at Jerry's Deli in Beverly Hills would give me so many gifts in the years to come. Beauty doesn't mean a damn thing if you don't know your worth.

We hope you don't stay with someone not worthy of your time because *we* know what you are worth. But to say you should or should not X, Y, and Z would send a message that there is something wrong with you and your experiences. Our past "disasters" are how we got here; our past no's turned into our one undeniable yes. Our life story *is* who we are. Do we have regrets? ABSOLUTELY! Don't we wish we spent the years we were focused trying to get the guy of the moment creating an actionable plan for our *own* life instead? Or at least reading some good fiction books and traveling while we obsessed? Hell yes. But we didn't, and here we are, with you. We wouldn't trade that for anything.

Worry less about what others think and more about what YOU think. Does that feel like an impossible feat because you have bossy BFFs? We have found that setting up our girlfriend calls with pre-warnings like these really helps us:

- I need to vent, not looking for advice.
- I really need to talk without any judgment.
- Hey, just a clearing-my-mind talk.

This helps most with friends who love to "help" and "fix." We must teach people how to treat us, and this includes our friends. We need to have boundaries on what does and doesn't work for us. If asking for advice always leaves us feeling judged by a particular friend, don't ask that person for advice! This book's principles can seep into and transform all areas of your life—if you use them.

We innately start going where the love is, and we must know what works and what doesn't—FOR US! When we do, we begin to prioritize our individual needs, must-haves, desires, and decisions. And *only you* can do that for yourself. It's been about you all along!

CHAPTER TWENTY-SEVEN

MAN-TRA
(IF YOU DARE)

This chapter may seem a little too simple—so much so that you may want to skip past it or only haphazardly give it a go. If the latter is the case, beware. We suggest you *only* take on this directive if you're willing to lose a guy should it turn out that being with him is not in your highest good. Of course, this is excellent news if you do indeed lose him because it means you're one step closer to someone who *is* your guy. That said, we certainly know that losing someone you don't yet truly know you don't want can be very painful.

As a human being, you have free will. However, there is a greater force we cannot control. Call it whatever you want. Try to fight it, but it's hard to deny. While this may sound a little bit too woo-woo to some, we promise you don't have to be a spiritual master to take this on. You simply need to listen to that small part of you that knows there is something outside of you that is more in charge than you are. Basically, if you can't stop a rainstorm (and you know it), you understand this principle.

Back to free will. If you don't give that force bigger than you an invitation to assist, things will continue progressing as they are.

But…

If you ask for help or a sign, you will absolutely get one. Keep in mind, what you're praying and asking for might yield results that you believe suck. But again, what are you willing to let go of to get what you want?

There is a mild version and a spicy version of the man-tra. If you want to tread slowly and gently, we suggest starting with the mild version. Unless, that is, you're ready for the truth, no matter how swift and harsh it may be.

The term man-tra was coined when Sara was working with a girl in a coaching program. While taking her through the generically titled "man prayers," her client brilliantly referred to it as "the man-tra" (thanks, Jenn!).

The spiritual healer Sara saw many years ago suggested that she ask the universe to help her. Her direction seemed simple enough, and so off she went with a basic prayer to use when and if she wanted. That evening while walking her dog, Sara looked up at the bright moon and said, very nonchalantly, "Hey, Universe. I really want X to be my guy. But if he is not in my highest good and divine purpose, if he is NOT the guy for me, block him and remove him from my life. Thank you! From me, Sara, in Los Angeles."

Note: This is the short form, very spicy version. The kicker: Sara was feeling pretty damn confident that things were looking really great, and that this would prove he was her guy.

We kid you not, later that night they had a fight they never recovered from. It was almost as if the wizard behind the curtain screamed, "MOVE, MOVE, MOVE NOW! FAST, SHE GAVE US AN IN...GO!" Relationship over.

That prayer has since morphed into fancier versions and has been used by hundreds of women. Sometimes the relationship got better, and the guy remained. Occasionally, he would return, or the romance would dissolve—sometimes immediately and other times slowly. But either way, the truth was shown.

The man-tra is powerful. You are giving whatever powers that be permission to *show* you the truth. Are you ready? Are you willing? Are you at that place where you just need to know once and for all? If so, you may be prepared to use the man-tra.

The first man-tra is the milder of the two. Use this if you are looking for a gentler response (even though we call this the mild man-tra, it can still feel abrupt).

MAN-TRA (mild)

"Universe/God/Goddess (fill in whatever name you prefer when it comes to the force of the universe) and all the powers that be,

I want to thank you for your help. I am in love with (or crazy about) ____, and I really want him to be my guy. I would love to end up with him and want him to be The One! I am asking you to show me the truth with him. If he is not the one for me and is not here for my highest good, show me the truth. Show me the signs clearly and directly. If he is meant for me, our relationship will flow smoothly and effort-lessly.

I am ready to know.

Thank you for your guidance and help."

If you are ready to take it a notch higher and would like to try a spicier man-tra, there are a few adjustments.

MAN-TRA (spicy)

"Universe/God/Goddess (fill in whatever name you prefer when it comes to the force of the universe) and all the powers that be,

I want to thank you for your help. I am in love with (or crazy about) ____, and I really want him to be my guy. I would love to end up with him and want him to be The One! I am asking you to show me the truth about us. If he is not the one for me, if he is not here for my highest good and divine purpose, then BLOCK him and show me obvious signs that I can't doubt. Show me the truth. If he is meant for me, let it flow quickly and effortlessly. If it is *not* meant to be, don't.

Thank you for your guidance and help."

Now, if you are currently not with your guy but really want to be, try this version:

MAN-TRA (breakups)

"Universe/God/Goddess (fill in whatever name you prefer when it comes to the force of the universe) and all the powers that be,

I want to thank you for your help. I am in love with (or crazy about) ____, and I really want him to be my guy and for us to get back together. Though I would love to end up with him and want him to be The One, I am asking you to continue to show me the truth about us. If we are meant to get back together, he will flow to me easily and effortlessly. If he is not meant to come back into my life, thank you for continuing to block him. I want him back, but only if he is here for my highest good and divine purpose.

Thank you for your guidance and help."

There you have it. Use these man-tras with caution and purpose. If you casually utter one while mopping up cat pee, *you* may not believe in its efficacy. And though that would most certainly be enough for the universe, we strongly suggest you make it official when you do it. Perhaps light some incense or a candle or go out into nature and be fully present for your statement.

Also, only do it when you're ready. If you are currently unable to see the truth, that's okay. These mantras aren't going anywhere. Do the man-tras seem too simple? Do you not like the way they are written? Is one not perfectly fitting your situation? If that's the case, tweak it to your liking. Do you know how many versions of these statements we have sent up with a flair? (Too many to count.)

Make sure you get straight to the heart of the matter: SHOW ME THE TRUTH ABOUT ___.

And, if you dare…

BLOCK HIM IF HE IS NOT THE ONE FOR ME.

Then pay attention.

Jacqueline's Story

It was right after Brookes told me that it was too soon after his divorce to really dive into a full-blown relationship (it took fifteen months of "us" for him to figure that out) that I began dating differently. It was a painful lesson. I decided that I was not committing to anyone until I knew he was The One. Thirteen dating apps can produce a massive number of prospects in Los Angeles, let me tell you.

Within three weeks, I was set for my third date with four exceptional prospects who had been incredibly consistent—texting, calling, and otherwise checking in every day. There was no room for anyone else, but I saw my college boyfriend on Match.com and agreed to dinner.

And then there were five.

I had to figure it out; it was becoming too much. I decided to ask the universe, with all sincerity, "Universe, help a girl out. If any of these guys is NOT for me, remove him/them!" Sometimes I forget how fast the man-tra works. I was stunned.

That week I was ghosted, stood up, and ignored. I never heard from any of them again, except my college love. I asked, and there he was...for the next three years. He ended up not being The One, but my relationship with him was life changing.

CHAPTER TWENTY-EIGHT

BUT...BUT...BUT...

We know you (once again) have a list of objections you have been patiently waiting to express. You've been taking notes, and you've no doubt developed some pretty intricate questions/concerns/debates in your head. In this chapter, we will address those loose ends flying around, pronto! We want you to feel heard and (hopefully) get all your answers.

Here we go...

"But...He's shy."

Maybe he is, but no amount of shyness will keep a guy from you if he wants you. We know we have mentioned the shy man before, but they are so often handled like precious newborn kittens, and they are not that. We have seen "shy" men pop out of their seats and chase women down the block. Sara once had a shy and homeless man (covering both categories of shy *and* down on his luck) interrupt her conversation to ask her out...repeatedly. Shy women may let certain things pass them by, but a shy man will not let a woman pass him by, or he won't allow it for long, anyway.

Men and women don't handle shyness in the same way. There are, of course, truckloads of loopholes offered regarding shy men. "My cousin is so awkward he can't ask anyone out, and he has never had a girlfriend." We don't *not* believe you, but we also have not seen a man deny at least an attempt to get to a woman he likes. That said, we know many women who believe a man passed her up because he was shy. Look, if he wants you, he will come to get you. If he doesn't try, he didn't care enough. Period.

"But...he's down on his luck."

While this objection could be tucked in nicely with "He's shy," we felt it deserved a stand-alone shout-out. Women have bent over backward (*ahem*, Jacqueline) for this one. "Oh, he was fired a year ago, so he can't take me to dinner or buy me a birthday present. I'll just take him to Fiji and send him Postmates every second day. Or maybe he isn't taking me on a date because he's poor. I'll make it easy and go to his house every day from here on out. I'll take him out to dinner and pay every time."

The worst thing that a man can have taken from him is his dignity. If he is genuinely down on his luck, you can definitely be respectful. In other words, don't demand a birthday dinner at The Four Seasons or the like. But don't rush in to fix or rescue him and his situation, either. He will (and needs to) figure it out on his own. He was fine before he met you, and he will continue to be fine. LET HIM BE! If he is interested in you, he will manage with what he has. Allow him to and thank him. That is what he wants. He doesn't want your assistance (even if he lets you provide it).

P.S. If he asks you for help, he may be a player and/or a taker. Run!

"But…he's been hurt before."

Provided you are over the age of twelve, who hasn't? Haven't you been hurt before? Perhaps you're hurting now! Yet here you are working on yourself. Yes, people can choose fear over love, but is that really your guy? Don't you want someone who is scared but does it anyway? If a man is into you, he will run straight into the fire. There is no need to toss cushions before him so he can walk towards you shrouded in a gentle cloud of safety. Don't forget that men are hunters and warriors by nature.

"But...he doesn't trust easily; he is cautious and wounded."

Same issue, different flavor. Okay, it is time for the story of all stories. Sara was "dating" a sexy comedian years ago. Dating is a strong word; they were "friends." Sara was crazy about him, but he was that edgy and wounded type, so she made sure to appear as that carefree, cool girl—the one who despises drama. She didn't want to spook him.

Long story short, one day, he announced over breakfast that they couldn't make out anymore because he now had a girlfriend. Apparently, a girl he liked in Vancouver suddenly became available. He got in his car and drove *through the night* from Los Angeles to be with her. This story has led to the belief that "a man will drive through the night for the girl he wants." There's no need to always "act" right. They will do what they want to do regardless.

"But...it's the 21st century; I can do what I want."

You are correct. You *can* do what you want. We *want* you to do what you want. But if you are open to change, and if you can hear your gut whispering that the information in this book rings even a little bit true, what do you have to lose by trying it? You can always go back to being in charge.

Men are different from women. This is as true now as it was in Roman times. Sure, they are a little more spoiled now, but a man's DNA is and will always be that of a hunter. Yes, women can also love hunting. (We wouldn't know personally because of the whole vegan thing. Have we mentioned this already?) Still, we are talking about the general nature of man versus woman. Ignore if you like or give it a try.

"But...I can't choose who I fall in love with."

Hmmmm... We don't want to downplay love. Love *is* love, after all. We don't care who you love, and we genuinely mean this. But is your love story really love? Before you throw this book into the fireplace, hear us out. Scan your life and look back on all those "soul mates." The one you met at Burning Man, the asshole from that fraternity in college, and that boyfriend with the wandering eye. See them all in your mind's eye. How many of them were really true love? Not obsession, not lust, not a challenge but REAL TRUE LOVE.

Exactly.

There's a big difference between a real love story and guys who aren't worth your energy, heart, or tears. So, we must ask, are you *certain* you're dealing with real love and not a life lesson?

"But...I don't believe there should be rules when it comes to love."

We couldn't agree more. There shouldn't be. Think of these suggestions less as "rules" and more as shifts in perspective, as new ways of looking at things with a more open mind. Let's use traffic as an example. Yes, you are totally free to drive down the wrong side of the road. You can speed and risk the lives of others. You can even spit out of your window, freaking people out, whenever you want. You can continue speeding and spitting for as long as you want—until you get pulled over and cited.

When it comes to love, you can create wreckage, but the worst damage is the damage that you do to yourself. It is not our intention to turn you into a law-abiding love citizen, but instead of scoffing at dating rules, perhaps look at them as other people's errors and lessons being put to good use.

"But...If I were only prettier, sexier, or skinnier, he would love me."

We spent a whole chapter on this, but it is worth repeating. You will not have to bend over backward for your guy—people like who they like, whether they're in sweats or a bikini. If you knew that your grandma hated pitted fruit, you would perhaps bring her a key lime pie, even though you would rather the peach, no? You would roll with the lime version because you knew it was her thing, right? It doesn't mean that there's something wrong with a peach. You may even think, "Who doesn't love a peach?" Grandma, that's who.

It's the same with so-called "types" people fight against, trying to defy logic. Before you sign up for that 5am boot camp, ask yourself if you are doing it because you love getting up at dawn and being yelled at to run by a former marine turned personal trainer. Or, are you doing it to look a "certain way" to get the guy.

"But...he is now in therapy and swears he will never cheat again."

Wonderful. There are success stories out there, and people do change if they really, really want to. Enough about him, however. Can *you* forgive him? Can *you* not live with the paranoia that he will do it again? Can *you* forgive the past? Can *you* own the choice that he is worth the risk? If the answer is a heartfelt yes, good! Whether or not he is truly genuine can only be seen between the two of you and over time. Some people are more open to things than others, and if you can see his humanity in this instance, then trust it (but re-read chapter 23: Know Mr. Wrong from Mr. Wrong).

"But...this time is different."

Gosh, we hope so. While it's working out, it doesn't hurt to practice letting go of any ideas, thoughts, or plans that tell you that you have to *do* something specific to get him to commit with ease. If it's different this time, it will flow so beautifully that you won't need to prove it, to us, to others, and most of all...to yourself.

"But...my psychic and/or astrologer confirmed that we are destined."

You can put those hundred dollars back in your purse; we're telling you this for free (or a small fee if you have purchased this book). We don't care if your moons align or your Venus is kismet or your psychic talked to your grandfather on the other side, and he agrees. If your guy is not calling, not committing, and not moving mountains to make you his when he knows someone else could swoop in and grab you, he is "at this time" not destined for you. This isn't to say that he won't ultimately realize what he has with you and come running. But if he is currently MIA, there is nothing to do except take that focus and put it on yourself.

"But...I can't focus, and I can't think of anything but him."

Ugh. This is the question of all questions: "How do I focus on me when all I can think of is him: his call, his intentions, and what he will do?" What if there is no perfect answer? What if you just do the best you can? Isn't thinking of him *while* you try to focus on writing that novel or signing up for a class or visiting your mom better than not doing these things? We have yet to snap a finger and "stop it," as many well-meaning friends and professionals have suggested. Have you? If you can't "shake him off," try letting that be okay, and make an effort to *also* do you.

P.S. You're awesome.

"But...men have fought wars for love. It shouldn't be trivialized in this book."

Exactly. They have. Is he fighting for you? Things have indeed changed since The Trojan War, so let's put it in perspective. Is he lifting that very, very heavy smartphone to shoot off a text to you?

"But...there's more. What about...?"

The buts can go on forever. There is always a "but." But...is he in your life? If he is, is he trying? Do you have to continually tell him what he should or should not be doing? Are you happy? Does he try? If he isn't in your life but you're left wondering, what are you not seeing? We spend so much time focused on how *he* should be that we can overlook elementary things.

Is he TELLING you who he is, but you do not want to believe it? (Refer to chapter 16: Pay Attention To Patterns.)

Are you focused on someone who isn't giving you what you really deserve? Have you been settling for scraps? (Refer to chapter 9: You Cannot Lose What's Yours.)

Do you think that outside circumstances are getting in the way? That it would work if only your BFF would stop unknowingly flirting? If he could only get over his ex. (Refer to chapter 5: Even Giselle Bundchen Wouldn't Change Him.)

WHATEVER YOUR "BUT" IS, it can be remedied by one simple realization: This was never about him; it was always about *you*! If you are ninety percent obsessed, put ninety percent of your focus on something that will lift you up. If you are fifty percent angry, then take that energy and release it or put it into your passions. If you are twenty percent wounded as you walk through life, take that twenty percent, double it, and show up for someone else who is wounded.

We are not trying to be martyrs or annoying optimists; that kind of behavior is eye-roll worthy. However, if you are disturbed or thrown off by something outside of you (like him and what he is doing or not doing), you can challenge yourself to one-up it and pour more into your own life, flaws and all, pain and all, frustration and all! Trust us, it's worth the risk.

Take in ALL of the situation and all your past hurts and use them to *magnify you!* That's something previous relationships *did* give to you! They brought you here. How perfect is that?!

CHAPTER TWENTY-NINE

FOR THE FEMINISTAS

Dear Feministas,

There are as many variations of feminists as there are seasons of *Project Runway*. Within the feminist movement, there is discord on merely the definition of feminism, let alone how the concept should be embodied in society. Before we begin throwing our opinions into the mix of this highly debatable movement, we want to extend an overarching caveat. Similar to how we have written this book from the perspective of women dating men, we can discuss feminism from where we stand. We are White Western American women, and that is the only perspective we know. In other words, we realize that any conversation we incite from this position will come off as ethnocentric.

There are 195 countries globally, each possessing

its own history, biases, evolutionary development, and socioeconomic structures. We cannot, nor would we, presume to generalize for any of them. Nor can we generalize for women of color or differing religious affiliations, even within the United States. In fact, entire sects of feminism have been explicitly initiated to combat this problem. Please hear what we are saying with that in mind. Even Jacqueline, as a Woman's Studies minor (the irony is not lost on us), cannot encapsulate and summarize this movement.

We will offer you our simplistic and rudimentary perspective for this chapter's sake and what we wish to convey. There are many feminist viewpoints. Some acknowledge women and men are equal but should be treated differently, while others believe in the complete dismantling of the patriarchal system. Some wish to create a separate matriarchy, and others wish to remove the idea of any dominator, full-stop.

These varying concepts span all belief systems, including that biological sex doesn't influence gender in its most basic form. While we agree that it doesn't have to, we believe that there are inherent biological and physical differences that became part of the sexes' divergent fabric when combined with thousands of years of societal influence. In addition, there are many different types of feminism incorporating social status, race, and geographical differences, to name a few. For the sake of this book, we are operating under the generalized pretense that women and men have fundamental differences.

Paring down our ideas to the most fundamental belief on which we can all hopefully agree, we define feminism as standing up for women's overall empowerment—socially, politically, economically, racially, and religiously. Not unlike politics, you probably won't agree with everyone else's opinion or what's most important, even in (or at) your own party, but this is what makes life beautiful. At the heart of feminism is the passion and drive for the betterment of women. When we move past our differences, we can appreciate each other for the thread that connects us: love.

Can we agree on that? It's okay if we can't. Even the two of us have varying views when it comes to what feminism means. We don't have to align on every talking point, but we've found a way to write this chapter because we have a common underlying mission. And this message trumps any nitpicking. We want to empower and uplift women regardless of any storyline that told you that you weren't deserving of everything you desire in this lifetime. You can disagree with what we stand for, how we dress, or the way we talk or laugh. Still, if we can awaken you, via that guy that you really want, to the fact that YOU are worthy, impressive, beautiful, and deserving of magic, then we served a purpose in these pages.

The simplification of this idea (our empowerment and inherent worth) can become a unifier among us all. The world is divided among rights, wrongs, shaming, and cancel culture. Isn't life better *because* we all have different opinions, ideas, passions, and beliefs? Our thoughts and feelings vary on everything from dating to love to long-lasting mascara. There is room for all. Let's lift each other up and celebrate the joys of being a woman. It is a gift—for us and for the men we share the planet with.

So, what does feminism have to do with dating? Everything.

Because we observe and know many powerful women, we have witnessed something interesting: Not one has the same beliefs regarding dating as the next. Many believe that old-school dating "rules," per se, are outdated and unnecessary. We get the logic. When we were wild and young, we absolutely scoffed at any parental guidance on dating. But we aren't talking about young women only; we are talking about women of all ages. It's become an insult to the cause to fall prey to old ideas about love. "We are equal"—though absolutely correct and mandatory to respect—has almost overshadowed another truth: Men and women may be equal, but they *can* be different, and that is okay too.

It's the difference that holds the key.

We delved into this in chapter 13, so we won't repeat ourselves unnecessarily. However, we want to stress that you can still be a powerful badass *and* let that guy treat you like a queen. These two concepts are not mutually exclusive.

If it gives you great joy to be the breadwinner or run the show in your relationships, we also support that vision. *You get to choose.* No matter what you claim and own as your truth, we invite you to open your mind to an additional and different possibility —one that will compliment your powerhouse reality: Men are amazing too.

Sure, there are many assholes (we're sure we have dated most of them). But overall, men are doing the best they can, too: learning, growing, epically bombing at life, and *hopefully* becoming better for it. Additionally, suppose you possess a generalized hatred of the male population. In that case, you will make it really hard to manifest a kind, loyal guy. We never want to say it's impossible (as you clutch on to your loopholes for dear life).

You can consider yourself a feminist *and* love and respect men.

We do not turn a blind eye to bad behavior or anything else that doesn't honor our equality. Quite the opposite. We can shine, be brilliant, and conquer the world while we let them do the same. One does not take away from the other.

You do you; I'll do me.

Do we seem naive? Are men the problem, and we just can't see it? Are we not aware of all the shit they've collectively put us through? Here's the thing: We've seen it. We've done our hating and blaming. We've simply arrived at the other side and found that our most painful experiences were our experiences—not because of "men" in general. We did our work, and we healed.

Again, we are not naïve nor ignoring the appalling issues throughout the world involving sex (harassment, rape culture, sex trafficking, underage pornography, domestic abuse, to name only a few). We can only control our lives and our actions. As we each change individually, we can begin to shift and transform our surroundings. We believe in addressing outdated and harmful societal standards, but we must first work on ourselves.

That work may include temper tantrums, anger, or sadness; it's about *your* unique process. If you are pissed off, be pissed off. Own that! We want you to really let it out! Heal your heart. Then, when you are free, the pendulum can swing back to its proper place, and you will see that there are amazing men everywhere. And they want to make you happy (but your happiness is an inside job). They also want to fall in love and be monogamous and plan a wedding and have babies. They, too, want what you want. You just might not have seen them before.

We want you to find that man who adores you, and we know he's out there. The world is filled with beautiful souls if you focus on that. Anything else can be the lesson that got you to yours.

Love is always the way!

Sara's Story

I was in a coaching program study group recently. One of the girls recommended a dating book she loved, and another girl went off in the group the next day:

"Why is it always the women doing all the work to get the guy or trying to change? Why aren't they reading up on us? Why is it always us changing our behavior?"

I'm poorly paraphrasing, but the bottom line is, she was pissed. And it's true. It's always the girl clutching the crystal ball, endlessly analyzing his words or texts, who tend to go the extra mile for "him."

So, what if we just shift perspective a bit? Instead of getting mad and declaring, "Fuck that bullshit," when we realize this, maybe we just do what feels fun but add more of *ourselves* into the equation. What if nothing was lost? What if we learned that our tight new body that was inspired "for him" is really for ourselves? He was just the one who made it happen. When we get *there*, we have won.

Just a thought.

CHAPTER THIRTY

AN OPEN APOLOGY TO MILLENIALS

When we found out that the eggplant, water droplet, and peach emojis had become part of a new mating call or that guys were using an array of emojis to say, "Just come over," we were disturbed (to say the least).

We admit it. We had it wrong. We thought love and romance were going to be boxed up with all those old VHS tapes stored in your mom's attic when we had a conversation with a young millennial about said emojis and their meanings.

"But how do you date?"

"Date?" Followed by a long awkward pause. Then a laugh. "We don't date."

This was all very concerning. Sara, a casting director who also worked in development, quickly created a show: "How to Save the World, One Millennial at a

Time." It would be hilarious and show how courtship and dating should be done. She was sure it was a hit. Fast forward to an agent pitch meeting. The agent (probably a millennial herself) was not amused.

"Millennials wouldn't like this at all. It's saying they are doing something wrong."

Mind-blowing moment.

How many times do we need to hear the exact same thing: Millennials (and everyone else) do not want some patronizing martyr coming in to save them. Sara previously listened to the same pushback when working with someone in Africa on a few television show ideas. In fact, the first thing said to her in a meeting was, "As long as you aren't proposing something where you come in to save everyone. They don't need saving." This man explained how everyone he knew in Africa was more tech-savvy, stylish, and hip than he could ever be. To be clear, we are not saying that no one needs help. Of course, people need help, but that "Poor you, let me help you out" vibe is a buzz kill usually not well received. Sometimes people just want to have some damn fun!

Millennials can teach us so many things, from tech skills to forward-thinking vision and drive. You, in our eyes, are modern-day Feministas for real. You're powerful, quick, and have the skills and mindset to become CEOs before most of you graduate from college. You are quite literally the future. And, if we may say so ourselves, anyone who has grown up "online" deserves a reward period. You have thick skin and hearts of gold.

Our challenge to you is to consider these concepts. Try them out a little bit; put them to the test. We can achieve and be whatever we want, but sometimes when it comes to male and female relationships, we forget that a man still loves to chase and conquer.

There may be a "re-training period" if you are dealing with men who've been spoiled. It can be un-charted territory for many younger men, even though their hunting nature is in their DNA. They become accustomed to girls asking them out and making it easy. They now just lean back in that EZ chair and let the emojis flow. Suppose a one-emoji text gets a girl to his house without him having to lift a finger and dial a number. In that case, it may take a minute for him to realize what's happening.

BUT…

He will likely love it, even though he may not know what hit him.

A friend of ours has a very popular, gorgeous son and girls throw themselves at him repeatedly. His mother commented that the girl he liked was quick to ask him out. He said, "I hate it when they do that; I totally would have asked her out." He was no longer interested.

THEY WANT TO COME TO YOU!

Let them. If they don't come…well, we suggest you re-read this book to discover what that means!

Dive into other relationship books as well. We are sure you will find the cool modern version on making it all work out while incorporating emojis. Remember, we may have just moved into the age of Aquarius, but we are still only human beings. Older books, new books, even a meme on Pinterest—if it resonates with you, it is speaking the truth for you.

When a young millennial friend was having a hard time with a crush, we suggested she read an old classic: Men Are from Mars, Women Are from Venus, and she called later that day to say, "Ohmygod, I feel like I found the meaning of life. Everything makes sense. I've seen the light."

The shock to us was the speed at which she read. "Oh, no," she clarified. "I listened to the audio version at 3X the speed."

Millennials are brilliant.

CHAPTER THIRTY-ONE

AS WE PART WAYS

Midway through this book, it was likely quite apparent that we would not be recommending best practices for Tinder swiping. We didn't have a secret stash of how-tos for you to implement to obtain that five-carat ring on Christmas Day and waltz down the aisle the following summer. We haven't included a step-by-step guide on irresistible blow jobs that will keep him interested for the long haul.

But there was *one* detail permeating every page and echoed by each chapter. It is the component you forgot, the one we *all* ignore, the one that is and has always been the most valuable part of all: This was never about him. It was about YOU!

Every "him" brought you back to you. And for that priceless gift, let's take a moment and thank him (inside your head, don't reach for that phone). Whether it took twenty days or twenty years of pure, full-throttle focus on "him" to get you here, now is perfect. There is no missing time, only missing perception.

You were right on schedule. He was right on schedule. Whether he is currently in your life or not, know that unnecessary focus on him merely provides a delay in focusing on YOU!

We know. This is a thoroughly annoying summation of all these pages. When we were in the thick of it with this or that guy, crying, begging, praying, and dreaming it would work out exactly how we wanted, the *last* thing we wanted to hear was that *he* was not the point. That he didn't matter. If you had hit us with that line of reasoning early on in our own journeys, you might have gotten a swift kick to the head. We only wanted him. The fix. The answer. The One. That was the only acceptable outcome. So, thank you very much, but we were not concerned with our job, a new script, taking a class, or focusing on our gifts and skills. We wanted what we wanted: *that* guy and *that* relationship.

It's embarrassing to admit but true. That was our focus: Will he call? Will he come back? Does he love me? We were barely an afterthought in our own lives. As strong women, we don't want to admit to that type of external fixation. But here we are.

Please hear us: This isn't—and never was—about *him*. Focus on what *you* want in *your* life.

Perhaps you've reached this last chapter thinking, "What the fuck? There were no actual, clear rules in here to follow." And you would be correct. We didn't intend to provide clear-cut rules. We don't know what you are meant to learn or when you are meant to learn it. Let's take ourselves, for example. Sara was one to make and adopt rules quickly, while Jacqueline embraced them slowly. Does that mean one approach was better than the other? No. Who acts as both the judge and the jury? YOU! If you discovered lessons, meaning, growth, and most importantly, yourself, it was time well spent. We wouldn't want any "rules" to circumvent your biggest leaps forward.

We want you to be empowered to do whatever you want to do. Stay for ten years, marry him, leave him—all are acceptable answers. But one thing you *must* do is accept him for who he is, hear what he tells you, and believe what he shows you. As long as your eyes are open and you're willing to own your choices, go for it.

Fifteen years ago, a girl said to Sara, "I feel like you think everything is okay." She was implying that she could murder someone, and it would roll off Sara's back. She missed the point of Sara's absence of judgment when it comes to other people. It wasn't about whether or not Sara had an opinion on whatever action someone took. It was that she knew that people *could* do whatever they wanted to do if they were willing to own the consequences of their choices.

We don't know what someone's path is supposed to be, but we would like to keep you from going down roads that may cause you pain —if you don't have to go down them. We are eternally grateful we didn't fight for a fill-in-the-blank asshole from 2002, but that same asshole may be someone else's most powerful life lesson.

We would love for you to believe what our experiences have laid out, but only you can apply any of them to your life. We hope "he" comes back, and you run off into the sunset together. We really, really do. But if you are reading this, then at some point, you've wondered, waited, and questioned. And so, what do you have to lose by trying something different?

It's scary to let go and see if someone wants to be in your life by his own choosing, with no ties and no obligation. He could leave. Or come back. Or both. It is a risky proposition, but continue to ask yourself, "What am I willing to let go of to get what I want?"

We want these pages to sink into you and change you from the inside out because we have seen how it has transformed so many women, including ourselves. We are not clairvoyant. We don't know if a guy will or will not stay, come back, or move to Australia. Love, chemistry, and jobs all fall into that category of universal logic. Some things are just out of our control, like the ocean tides and thunder. Because of this lack of control, hope is everything. Hope gives us each the freedom to loosen the grip on what we think we want.

JUST KNOWING THAT HE COULD COME BACK OR STAY IS OFTEN ALL THE MOTIVATION WE NEED TO LET GO.

We had to turn over the fear a little. Trust that it could work out. Or not. And if it didn't, we had to trust that we would get something even better. If we were told, "Think these things! Do it right! Don't screw up!" we wouldn't have done a damn thing differently.

So, yes, this was all about you this entire time. Subconsciously you knew that, but we just needed to shift and maneuver you a little bit so you could see it clearly. We needed to remind you that freedom is our true nature, and if we are truly free, we can allow other people to be free. At that point, we'll have no doubt.

The essence of this book is freedom. Everything that you need, want, and cling to is what you need to let go. It's annoying to say, but it is all an enormous surrender. That said, what stays is worth it! May you be loved as fiercely as you can love yourself.

Sara's Story

Looking back, I notice that my long-term relationships (and now marriage) fell into place quickly. Effortlessly. I didn't doubt or overthink or ask fourteen friends what they thought. It just was. This doesn't mean it's the same for everyone, but it's worth noting in my case.

All those guys who I cried, worried, and tripped over didn't stick. Believe me, at the time, I wanted them to, but they didn't. Is that coincidence? Perhaps. Or is it: "When something is, it just fucking is."

I never considered myself a dating expert. If anything—outside of my usual occupation as a casting director for reality television—I would claim the role of female empowerment coach long before claiming to be a dating expert. Hey, maybe I can finally use that firewalking certification that's sitting in my closet somewhere. I love uplifting women. But one day, I read an essay by Mark Manson titled "The Most Important Question of Your Life," in which he talked about what we actually do versus the fantasy of what we think we want to do. My immediate reaction:

"Dammit, I want to be a screenwriter, but all I really do is talk to girls on the phone all day about guy issues." Thanks, Mark.

I then looked back at my hobbies over the previous decades (yes, decades). I had a career and some sub-careers, but dating talk was the one thing I did without fail—all day, every day. I spent thousands of hours listening to women ask, "Where is he, and does he care?"

Here's the whole story in a nutshell. Though I was partying like it was 1999, I entered 2000, the turn of the century, in heartbreak. Way back when, in the days of phone booths and Thomas Guides, I had a terrible breakup. I was crushed, and I had no idea what to do with the pain. I was loaded with way too many feelings I had no idea how to handle. Somehow, I made my way to a spiritual teacher whom I saw three times a week for a year. I noticed that whenever I went to her, I felt better, so I just kept going. My goal was to "get him back," but what happened instead was a slow shift in my thought processes.

While much of what you read in this book came from my time spent with that spiritual teacher, I started collecting other ideas along the way. Because I am a bad student, I morphed them into my own, and I'm sure I did them "wrong," but they worked. Then I met another spiritual teacher later in the 2000s who expanded my thoughts in a completely different direction. If you can't already tell, I am a shopper, but instead of shoes, I like ideas, and teachings, and aha moments that change me at my core. These "ideas" became the topics of my conversations with friends, and often they'd gift them to their friends. I became the one people called when dealing with "guy stuff."

I got a job in reality television and have worked on many dating shows. But in my free time, I would talk with women about their dating woes, day and night. And then I met my husband, after which point it occurred to me that I should write these ideas down in a book, which I did in 2007 but did nothing with it.

Then in 2013, my BFF Jacqueline and I thought it would be fun to revamp it, which we did, but we still didn't put it out. More recently, a writer friend of mine said during a phone call, "It's selfish to deny the world your book." I had these tried-and-true ideas, and they worked. If they helped me and many I know, they might help someone I don't know as well, and that is all that matters.

Sara is a Casting Director for reality television (NBC, Bravo, Playboy, WEtv, MTV, BET, VH1, and more) and some movies ("Death Link", "Just Swipe", "Wolf Mountain"). She writes about love, codependency, vibration, and all things growth. She is also the author of the illustrated female empowerment book, *There is a Woman.*

Jacqueline's Story

Hopefully, as you've arrived at the close of this book, it's painfully clear that one of us followed these suggestions, got married, and was determined to impart the wisdom of her ways to thousands of women. The other didn't. (That would be me.)

I always desperately wanted a partner, starting back in the second grade when I fell madly in love with Ariel Scott Menzel. Love notes, pleading eyes, and even begging were never out of the question or repertoire when it came to capturing his attention. Alas, it never worked. And the degree of dependence I had on having whoever the "him" of the moment was—being good enough, thin enough, and perfect enough—dug a deeper and deeper hole within me, one that could only be (temporarily) filled by the next "him." It was a vicious cycle.

I heard Sara's words. I saw her take action, change, and meet her husband. But more importantly, I saw her refuse to be unwavering in her self-esteem. Nevertheless, I had what I believed was a better idea—and when I say better, what I really mean is, I wanted to do it my way. I did everything OTHER than what is suggested in this book because I wanted the outcome that I wanted. As a result, I ended up with men who cheated, felt insecure around, who left, who couldn't commit—or who wanted to commit immediately and then left. With every man I refused to let go of, a little piece of me broke.

I did it my way until the thought of doing it my way one more time was so thoroughly exhausting that I acquiesced. You cannot fake true surrender. Sometimes it arrives after complete decimation, but when it does, it's beautiful. Dating with my eyes open, self-worth intact, and no desperation is quite a different experience. My crazy, book-worthy dating excursions have come to an end after a good twenty-five years, and the peace I exchanged it for was well worth it.

I was messy, sometimes even pathetic. But those behaviors got me to the place I needed to be to let it go. I couldn't have done it any other way at that point, and trust me, I tried. Perhaps after reading our experiences, you have been imbued with a small amount of hope that you don't have to continue doing things that make you angry, frustrated, sad, or feeling desperate.

I have finally met someone kind, emotionally available, and generous of spirit, time, and love. I may be with him for another year, and I may be with him for the rest of my life. Maybe it will end, or maybe we will be married before you close the book. But it doesn't matter. Because I'm free, happy, and secure, and that's all I was trying to feel the entire time anyway.

In addition to all things love, Jacqueline's primary

mission is saving animals. She is a Board Member at the Material Innovation Institute and serves as Senior Advisor for The Good Food Institute and FFAC. She was featured on CNN and in the documentary "Explant" for her experience with the BRCA gene. She is also a contributor to *The Huffington Post* and other publications.

Made in the USA
Las Vegas, NV
20 January 2022

41832656R00157